The Accidental Manager

The Accidental Manager

surviving the transition from professional to manager

SHEILA UDALL and
JEAN M. HILTROP

PRENTICE HALL

NEW YORK LONDON TORONTO SYDNEY TOKYO SINGAPORE
MADRID MEXICO CITY MUNICH

First published 1996 by
Prentice Hall Europe
Campus 400, Maylands Avenue
Hemel Hempstead
Hertfordshire, HP2 7EZ
A division of
Simon & Schuster International Group

© Prentice Hall Europe 1996

Typeset in 11/12 pt Baskerville
by Photoprint, Torquay, Devon

Printed and bound in Great Britain by
T. J. Press (Padstow) Ltd

Library of Congress Cataloging-in-Publication Data

Udall, Sheila
    The accidental manager : surviving the transition from
professional to manager / by Sheila Udall & Jean M. Hiltrop.
        p.   cm.
    Includes bibliographical references and index.
    ISBN 0–13–362849–3
    1. Executives. 2. Management. 3. Professional employees.
4. Career development.   I. Hiltrop, Jean M. (Jean Marie)
II. Title.
    HD38.2.U3   1996   95–25095
    658.4–dc20   CIP

British Library Cataloguing in Publication Data

A catalogue record for this book is available from the British Library
ISBN 0–13–362849–3

---

1 2 3 4 5   00 99 98 97 96

Contents

List of figures

About the authors

SHEILA UDALL, MA is an independent training consultant with twenty years' experience in management training and development both in the public and private sectors. Starting her career as a training advisor in the engineering industry, she has also taught Human Resource Management at postgraduate level and been Deputy County Training Officer in a major local authority before starting her own business in 1989.

She has been involved in developing innovative strategies for management development in many large organizations as well as the National Health Service and local government. Since obtaining an MA in Organizational Psychology at Lancaster University, much of her work has focused on the issues involved in changing the culture of organizations, particularly helping people with professional backgrounds to develop managerial approaches and skills. She has co-authored two previous books, *People and Communication* (with Rita Udall, Hulton, 1979) and *The Essence of Negotiation* (with Jean Hiltrop, Prentice Hall, 1995).

JEAN M. HILTROP, Lic., MBA, PhD is Professor of Human Resource Management at the International Institute for Management Development (IMD) in Switzerland. He has been involved in executive education for many years at the Management Centre of the University of Bradford, at the Lovanium International Management Centre and at the Katholieke Universiteit Leuven in Belgium. He has worked as a human resource manager and consultant for several large companies in Europe, Asia and the United States.

His most recent publications include *European Human Resource Management in Transition* (with Paul Sparrow, Prentice Hall, 1994) and *The Essence of Negotiation* (with Sheila Udall, Prentice Hall, 1995). He is currently leading an international research project, which examines the impact of human resource practices on the global strategy and competitiveness of organizations.

Acknowledgements

To all those managers, colleagues, students and workshop participants who have been willing to share their experiences, concerns and ideas with us.

To our families and friends for their continued patience, encouragement and support.

Introduction

The problem is that people have to be frightened enough to believe they have to change, and then encouraged enough to believe they can.

(CIVIL ENGINEER/MANAGER 1993)

The story of Joe

Joe Jones works for Jordan Engineering, a company which manufactures electronic equipment for the power industry. It was founded in 1980 and quickly grew from a UK base to sell its products into Europe and subsequently the Middle and Far East. Operating in a competitive market, the company's success was built on innovative research and development (R & D) and a closely knit management team who worked well together and so were able to make rapid decisions. As the company developed, however, it also became less flexible. It was organized into the traditional functions of R & D, production, finance, sales and personnel, and it became more difficult to gain agreement for new initiatives from the heads of all these departments.

By the late 1980s the company was feeling the effects of the economic recession in Britain, but despite strong competition from the Far East managed to sustain its overseas markets and consequently its UK production. However, customers were becoming more demanding, wanting current products to be tailor made to their needs, backed up by a wider product range and better support services. It became crucial to learn more about the customers' businesses and develop new approaches including marketing.

Joe has been with the company from the start and was its top salesman. He loves selling and holds strong views about 'the right approach' to being a sales professional, which, to him, means building and keeping a good relationship with every customer. He is easygoing but persuasive and persistent, and has used his excellent interpersonal skills to gain the confidence of many sceptical buyers. He argues that you need to win the trust of the customer, listen to their concerns and then convince them that you have the right product to meet their needs. Once you have agreed one sale, then you need to keep in touch with regular visits and deals which made the customer feel 'special'.

His consistently good results led to promotion and within a few years he became the team leader, then the Sales Manager.

This meant that he had far less direct contact with customers and he did complain from time to time that he really missed them and the 'buzz' you got from a new deal, but Joe kept one or two key customers and continued to enjoy his job, until a new chief executive was appointed in 1994.

Ed Thomson was recruited from the United States to bring fresh ideas and drive to a company which had been relatively successful but still had outgrown its original management team, many of whom wanted things to be 'as they always had been' even though there was considerable evidence that the customers wanted a different approach. It soon became apparent that Ed wanted to make radical changes to the way the company worked based on his own management code of Direction, Accountability, Specialists and Teamwork. He established a new vision, new functions (including marketing), refined managerial and professional roles, and increased the use of new technology. He also instigated a change in recruitment practice to bring in highly qualified graduates with MBAs and MSc's. Great emphasis was placed on developing business and marketing strategies, and a new culture which expected professionals to work in creative, multi-functional project teams, focused on the market, while managers became team leaders and co-ordinators focusing on planning, solving problems and making decisions.

Early in 1995 Joe was promoted again to Marketing Strategy Manager. He did not really want the job but was 'encouraged' and 'expected' to take it. However, he did not thrive in his new role which was totally office based with no direct contact with customers at all, and at his last performance review Joe surprised his boss by saying that he was seriously considering leaving the company. 'It's all this paperwork, business plans, marketing plans, budget forecasts. I'm a salesman – my skills are in selling to customers not markets, these youngsters have no experience with people and I'm not cut out for this stuff. I've lost my enthusiasm. I seem to have very little in common with my colleagues any more, and my staff are bypassing me going straight to the project leaders. I'm left in a role which is not what I'm good at. It seems like I've ended up in this position by accident.'

The accidental manager

Are you one of the many people, like Joe, who start work in a given profession, undertake training and development, practise their skills and enjoy the work they have chosen, only to find that the only way to progress their career means moving away from the very thing they wanted to do to become a manager?

People move into a managerial role for a variety of reasons. For some the move is planned and welcomed, while for others it is done for less obvious reasons, certainly not from a basic desire to be a manager. Many people feel that they have little or no choice – they are expected to take the next step up even if that means away from the work they like doing and are good at.

Industry, commerce and, more recently, public sector organizations are increasingly subject to the 'managerial culture'. For scientists, engineers, doctors, computer technologists, accountants, teachers, social workers, architects, solicitors, probation officers, nurses, paramedics, sales professionals – in fact in almost every profession – building a career means that at some point you have to stop being a full-time professional and take on responsibility for managing other people.

This can lead to a number of uncertainties. You might be feeling any or all of the following:

1. *Uncommitted* to being a manager. How do you feel about taking on a wider responsibility than your professional work?
2. *Unclear* about what the role really entails. There are so many job titles and descriptions, what does being a manager in your organization really mean?
3. *Unsure* of your management skills. Many people say that in changing role they lose confidence in their abilities. Do you?
4. *Unwilling* to change. Would you rather stay on familiar ground and protect your professionalism?

These uncertainties can apply to people in all kinds of organizations, from small organizations to multinationals, from small professional practices to major consultancies, from hospital trusts to local authorities. The feelings are personal but they are also widely shared.

Who is this book for?

This book has been written for the following:

1. All those people who have already moved, or may soon move, into a management role from a professional role, and who feel that such a move is not specifically part of their career plan or one that they are entirely comfortable with.
2. Those people in organizations with responsibility for recruitment and promotion into managerial posts, including other managers or personnel professionals.
3. Anyone in a training, development and educational role who works with current or potential managers.
4. Those people in professional bodies who have responsibility for either the initial training or continuous development of their members.

How is the book structured?

The book is designed to be a practical guide. It is based on research with many managers who have identified approaches which did (or could have) helped them to make the transition from professional to manager a successful and enjoyable experience.

The book is also based on a metaphor – that of leaving a secure place, an island, and crossing a swamp to a new island, hoping that it offers the same kind of security but not really being too sure what to expect. It is also about the things that may help you in your journey across the swamp.

Chapter 1 The firm ground

In this chapter we explore what can provide you with the feeling of firm ground, or certainty, in your professional role and how the role of a manager is different. There are many theories of management but no guarantees – no one right way of ensuring success. There are also many myths about what managers do, but the reality varies so much for individuals and organizations that it is very difficult to develop a clear view of what to expect. It may be easier to know what you are leaving than what to expect, which is why it may feel like crossing a swamp.

Chapter 2 A view from the swamp

Many people appear to move into a management role as the result of a number of pressures. They may feel unsure about the role, confused and 'not in control' or 'floundering in a swamp'. At the same time the organization will frequently expect them to perform to a high standard immediately, but will provide little time or practical help for them to come to terms with a new set of responsibilities. In this chapter we ask the following: Are you in a swamp? What does it feel like? Can you go back? How might you go forward? What do you need to do?

Chapter 3 Letting go of the firm ground

The feeling of being in a swamp may, in part, be caused by being caught between two roles: not wanting to let go of one, nor fully embracing the other. Yet to take on a new role will almost certainly mean letting go of some of the 'hands on' elements of the previous one. You may have to stop doing some of the things that you really enjoy, for example, dealing with customers or working on the drawing board. More than that you may have to leave behind your professional identity from which you get recognition. We know that there are many factors which motivate people at work. If these factors have been linked directly to your professional role, then moving into management may mean losing them. So why change? We identify a number of benefits that a managerial role could offer to compensate you for what might be lost from a professional role and ask, which ones might encourage you to make the change? And, finally, how can you change?

Chapter 4 Testing the water

Being aware of your own attitudes to change is a crucial part of managing any new role. Your enthusiasm for meeting the challenges and developing new skills will depend to some extent on your attitudes to, and past experiences of, learning and change. There is increasing evidence that formal training (where it exists) cannot completely prepare you for the demands of a new role. In many instances it may be up to you to understand how you learn and to take the first steps in taking responsibility for your own learning.

Chapter 5 Swimming

At the same time you may have many skills which are transferable. If management is about 'achieving results through people towards organizational goals', managers from professions such as teaching and social work should have well-developed people skills, while those from science and engineering should be skilled in analyzing data and problem solving. What you will need to do is (i) use these skills in a different context, (ii) identify and develop additional skills and (iii) review and build such personal qualities as adaptability, resilience and leadership. The increasing use of competence-based development may be useful in this process. Can you identify, demonstrate and build on the competencies you already have?

Chapter 6 Stepping stones

There are a wide variety of organizational activities which can help you to survive the transition from one role to another. This chapter examines some of the things that can be structured into the way organizations work which can enable managers to become more effective, more quickly. These include having a clear organizational structure, good systems, specific personal objectives linked to performance review, together with good practice in recruitment, induction and training. It also invites you to review your own organization and how you might contribute to building these activities.

Chapter 7 Lifelines

Here we explore some of the more personal sources of help and support, which can also assist you in making the transition successfully. In the absence of stepping stones, individuals (including other managers) can offer such things as mentoring, coaching and feedback. Networks of colleagues can share problems, ideas and approaches, while counselling and stress management might also give an invaluable boost to your self-confidence in the short to medium term. What help exists? What could you develop for yourself?

Chapter 8 The new island: Managing in the year 2000

This chapter explores what it will be like managing in the foreseeable future. Many organizations seem to be experiencing fundamental and continuous change. 'Managing chaos' and 'managing turbulence' are terms being used to describe this process. What will the new management island look like? What skills will you need to be a successful manager in this situation?

Chapter 9 Are there any other islands?

What if, as a result of this exploration, you decide you do not want to be a manager? You may not want to go forward to this type of island, and you may not be able to go back to your professional firm ground. In this final chapter we explore some of the possible alternatives and invite you to reflect on your own values, needs and opportunities, in order to build the kind of future you want.

How to use the book

In our experience, busy managers rarely have the time to read a book from cover to cover and are usually looking for a practical rather than theoretical approach to their situation. You may want to read this book selectively, dipping into particular chapters or topics, and/or focus on the various questionnaires and activities to see how the issues relate to your own personal circumstances. To help you to do both of these we have organized each chapter to include the following:

- *An introduction* to the key issues.
- *Frameworks or theories* to explore the key issues.
- *Illustrations* in the form of quotes from practising managers (in boxes).
- *Questionnaires/activities* inviting you to analyze your own situation and/ or plan any action you may want to take.

Good luck! We hope you have a successful journey and enjoy your future role whatever it is.

Chapter 1

The firm ground

Let a man practise the profession which he knows best.
(CICERO 106–43 BC)

Introduction

Our starting point will be exploring the issues involved in changing roles. As we suggested in the introduction, like many other people, you may have started work in a particular profession because you wanted to work in that field, and/or develop and use your special interests and talents. You will probably have gone through extensive training to gain the necessary knowledge, skills and qualifications which provide the basis of a professional career. Once employed in an organization you will have learned what is expected of you, enabling you to be both competent and confident in your professional role. You may even have been able to progress within the profession and planned to carry on, and probably spend all your working life doing something you (a) enjoy and (b) are good at.

Then something happens, either the role changes due to circumstances outside your control such as re-organization or new legislation, or you have reached a limit and cannot stay in your professional role any longer. In order to progress you find that you need to move into a different role and take on managerial responsibilities.

What is the firm ground?

As Figure 1.1 shows moving into a management role means moving from the known or 'firm ground' of your strong professional base into less certain or 'swampy ground'. The sense of firm ground comes from many features of being a professional.

8

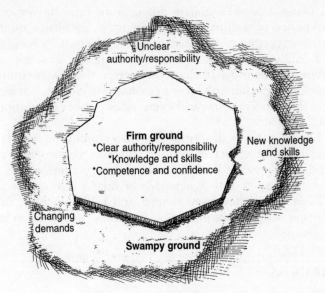

Figure 1.1   The firm ground

What is a 'professional'?

In sport, professional means 'not amateur'. To be professional means to be paid for an activity, but if we are thinking about professions such as medicine, architecture and engineering it would mean 'to have sufficient experience or skill in an occupation or an activity' and might include 'to be engaged in one of the learned professions – characterised by, or conforming to, the technical or ethical standards of a profession – characterised by conscientious workmanship' (Penguin Pocket Dictionary 1990).

Some occupations are clearly recognized as the traditional professions such as lawyers, doctors, and so forth. However, in focusing on these professions we would not like to exclude a number of other categories of work (such as administrators, salesmen and -women and computer technologists), where there is a clearly identifiable body of knowledge and skill, where people may have invested in lengthy training to gain qualifications, and where these people approach their work with as much commitment and 'professionalism' as those in the traditional professions. We are using the term professionalism in this context to refer to a set of characteristics or attitudes to work, against which individuals may be measured or assessed; these may extend to written codes of conduct or agreed and expected standards of behaviour, which are generally known and adhered to by the members of that profession.

Thus, being a professional is much more than having a job. The substantial period of training and experience to get formal qualifications that are widely recognized and accepted, together with a set of standards or code of conduct to work within, give you the 'firm ground'. This means having the confidence that comes from doing something you are capable of, which cannot only give personal satisfaction, but also respect from others for your expertise and even wider public recognition for your professional status.

This has also been described as the 'comfort zone'. If you are working well within your capabilities where there are clear guidelines and limited challenges it can begin to feel very comfortable, and you may not want to move into a new role or take a risk – a 'step into the swamp'. Even when they have moved and taken on new, managerial roles and responsibilities, some people find they must keep in touch with this 'firm ground'.

ILLUSTRATIONS

The Managing Director of a small engineering company was not in his office. Eventually he was found, working at a lathe in the factory. He came to a meeting reluctantly, saying 'I started this company to do what I like doing, making things. Now it is so successful that I don't get the chance to do that any more, and I really miss it. It has been a bad week so far, so I came in early to get back to my roots – the machines.'

A manager in public service (recalling when he was a newly appointed manager, and both he and his team were under a lot of pressure), 'So I got on with the case work, telling myself that the most helpful thing to do was pitch in and clear the backlog. Now I realize it was about my own comfort, in doing something familiar that I felt I was good at doing.'

There are many more examples, such as a computer manager writing and testing systems, a sales manager visiting known and valued customers and the engineer just doing something on the drawing board – all 'just keeping my hand in'.

Many professionals also belong to an association, a body of similarly qualified people who share common values and frequently have a real sense of pride in belonging to such a community. One of the advantages of having professional communities can be their role in upholding standards, but an equal disadvantage could be that sometimes professional bodies are felt to resist change and reject innovation. They can also be seen to promote exclusivity, and excessive pride in your own profession can lead you to denigrate other professional groupings or clients. Where this happens it means individuals can be resistant to change and therefore find it hard to move into other roles successfully.

ILLUSTRATIONS

A manager of a road maintenance team to a female training officer, 'You're not an engineer, dear, so you can't possibly understand my job.'

A manager/architect about the senior departmental manager, 'He's not an architect (so does not appreciate what I'm saying).'

How do managerial roles differ from professional ones?

Although several professions include management as part of their final qualification, there remains a lack of a precise definition of a manager. Even after decades of research and publications there appears to be no single, coherent definition or code of practice for effective management. Instead many theories of management exist side by side. This means there is little, if any, 'firm ground' for managers.

Henry Mintzberg (1973) took a more direct approach. He looked at what senior managers actually did. He identified a number of general characteristics of managerial work including the fact that managers perform a variety of roles, such as the following:

- Interpersonal roles – including acting as a figurehead for the organization, a leader of staff and liaison with other organizations.
- Informational roles – which mean acting as spokesperson for the organization and as a disseminator and monitor of information within it.
- Decisional roles – which include entrepreneurial activity, handling differences, allocating resources and negotiating within and outside the organization.

The study also showed that managers do the following:

- Perform a great quantity and variety of work at an unrelenting pace.
- Prefer issues that are current, specific and ad hoc.
- Sit between the organization and a network of contacts.
- Prefer verbal communication.

• Appear to be able to control their own affairs despite a 'preponder-ance' of roles, activities and obligations.

Most managers agree that these characteristics still describe their own work, with the notable exclusion of 'being able to control their own affairs'.

The changing role of managers

The research by Mintzberg and other writers has given us a clearer view of what it is *really* like to be a manager – a practical rather than theoretical perspective. Since the study was conducted, however, there have been major changes in the way organizations operate and, therefore, in the role of managers within them.

Scase and Goffee (1989) highlighted a difference between senior and middle/junior managers. Senior managers did receive substantial rewards and enjoyed the freedom of action and decision making, as described by Mintzberg. However, while middle and junior managers' roles shared the other characteristics, they did not share the freedoms. Instead their actions were increasingly subject to control by others, for example, by the use of job descriptions, performance monitoring/reviews and developing information systems to give accurate and current information about the individual and collective performance. Similarly, middle and junior managers may not see themselves as figureheads, having limited scope to make many decisions or allocate resources.

One reason for this development was that, up to the late 1980s, most organizations continued to grow and become more hierarchical, adding more management levels and functions to the structure. The image of the manager was as an 'organization man' (there were very few women in the role), who was expected to work all hours, be completely mobile, put the company first and give complete loyalty. In return these managers could expect good remuneration packages, security of employment and steady promotion/career prospects.

Since then the trend has reversed, and in the 1990s many organizations have moved to smaller business units, with greater flexibility, greater use of information technology, and a major focus on increasing productivity and cutting costs. In many cases this means that the role of managers (middle managers in particular) has changed dramatically. They now need to be more adaptive, be less committed to a career in one organization, have more varied patterns of employment and therefore be less psychologically immersed in the job. In addition, with the growth of opportunities for women in management, the need to manage dual careers has also emerged. All of which mean that it is virtually impossible to follow the sort of single 'planned career path' that may have been possible ten to fifteen years ago.

The future will inevitably involve even more changes in the managerial role. It seems that organizations will continue to change at an ever increasing rate. *Managing Chaos, Riding the Waves of Change* and *Managing in Turbulent Times* are typical titles of current management books. And yet at times it seems that the image of managers from the past has lingered, having produced a number of 'myths' which are still believed. Some of these myths applied to managers are the following:

- Managers work all hours.
- Managers must have the right answer to every question – now.
- Managers never take holidays, are sick or cannot cope.
- Managers are always in control.
- Managers have (all the) power.
- Managers never make mistakes.
- Managers are married to the company.
- Managers are never available; they are always in meetings.
- Managers get all the rewards.
- Managers interfere in everything.

Losing the firm ground

In reality many managers, particularly those who have come from a professional background frequently feel that they are not at all certain about their role and in particular how to manage staff.

The expectations that staff, colleagues and more senior managers have of you in your managerial role, may be very different from the expectations that your customers had of you in your professional role.

> **ILLUSTRATION**
>
> From head of physiotherapy, 'It's quite different being a manager. Staff question and challenge every suggestion I make – patients never did, they were just grateful for any help you could offer.'

You may also feel de-skilled and vulnerable, particularly if you have moved from a scientific or technical background, where you have been more accustomed to dealing with factual information and certainties, than the unpredictability of people.

ILLUSTRATIONS

During two separate courses exploring questioning skills for interviewing and appraisal:

A newly appointed production manager asked, 'How do you know what to ask second?'

A research chemist said, 'I can't do this kind of interviewing. I'm a scientist.'

Both managers were looking for the certainty that if they behaved in a particular way, or asked a specific question, they could predict/control the outcome of the interview.

Yet like many other managers, you may feel that you cannot talk about these concerns, at least not at work where, because of competition for promotion, it might jeopardize your career prospects. Instead you might deal with the pressures at home, with friends, or in other ways, including by distancing yourself from the problem – rejecting the need for a managerial role, perhaps even arguing that you do not need to be a manager because, as professionals, your colleagues are 'self-managing'.

ILLUSTRATION

The head of an architectural department, 'My staff do not need managing – we are all professionals.'

This can lead to a reluctance to take responsibility for planning, organizing and monitoring the work of others and, even more, a reluctance to delegate to staff work which you would rather be doing yourself. Given uncertainty about 'what the rules are' there can also be a real fear of failure.

To move from any one role to another involves uncertainty but to move from a framework of defined knowledge and skills, clear guidelines, codes of practice and well-known 'experts' to a management role may feel like moving into a swamp.

Questionnaire: Where is your firm ground?

Use the following questions to review how you see yourself and your current role. Do you see yourself as a professional and use that to provide the firm ground in your work? Do you see yourself as a manager? Or a combination of both? How does that feel?

---

1. What is your job title? Which role does it emphasize?
   (a) professional;
   (b) managerial;
   (c) both.

2. If you met a stranger at a party how would you describe what you do?
   (a) I am a professional;
   (b) I am a manager;
   (c) both (e.g. nurse manager or sales manager).

3. How do you spend your time at work?
   (a) with customers/on the drawing board/with a case load/teaching;
   (b) managing others;
   (c) a mixture of both.

4. Given a difficult professional issue, would you:
   (a) prefer to deal with it yourself?
   (b) work with a member of staff to decide what they should do?
   (c) work with the other person *and* get involved?

5. Given free time would you read:
   (a) a professional journal?
   (b) a management journal?
   (c) either or neither?

6. Do you ever find yourself defending your actions or attacking someone else's from a professional standpoint? (E.g. 'As a teacher, I would . . . .' or 'He's not an engineer, so. . . .')
   (a) yes;
   (b) no;
   (c) sometimes.

7. Given the opportunity to go on a training course, would you choose:
   (a) an area of professional interest?
   (b) a management skills course?
   (c) neither?

8. You are asked to be involved in the recruitment of a trainee in your professional area, would you want to talk with them about:
   (a) their technical ability?
   (b) their work experience and performance?
   (c) both?

9. Given the choice between two significant promotion opportunities, would you take:
   (a) a professional role?
   (b) a managerial role?
   (c) either?

10.   If you had a son or daughter would you try to influence their career
      choice into:
      (a)   your profession?
      (b)   a career in management?
      (c)   either or neither?

Interpreting your orientation.
If you score (a)s   You are on the professional firm ground.
If you score (b)s   You are on the management firm ground.
If you score (c)s   You are in transition.

(Use Figure 1.2 to indicate whether you are in transition.)

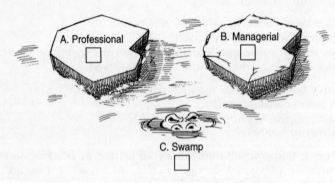

Figure 1.2   Are you in transition?

Chapter 2

A view from the swamp

*When you are up to your arse in alligators it is hard
to remember that your original objective was to drain
the swamp.* (SOURCE UNKNOWN)

Introduction

Why do people move into management?

We know that people move into managerial roles for many reasons. For
some people it is a planned and welcomed step in their career, but for
many other people it is more by accident than design. Some of the
reasons why people move into management are illustrated by the
following quotes:

ILLUSTRATIONS

- 'The only way to progress (climb the ladder) was to become a manager.'
- 'To improve my (the family) standard of living.'
- 'We needed the money.'
- 'I thought I can't do a worse job than X.'
- 'Frustration – you can only go so far in the profession.'
- 'If I didn't apply for the job X would.'
- 'I was expected to apply for the post.'
- 'To protect professional standards/values/principles.'
- 'To protect the staff/service/patients from people making decisions
  when they don't understand what we are really about.'

These quotes also demonstrate that although the move may not be
planned neither is it accidental in the sense of 'it just happened'.
Instead, people frequently feel under some sort of pressure to make the
change. The pressure can come from a personal basis such as to provide
increased income and/or security for yourself or a family, or can be work
based, such as an expectation from others that you will apply for the
next step up the ladder.

What are the pressures?

To improve your situation

You may feel compelled to continuously improve your position or your status. This may come from family values or learned definitions of success. For example, you must 'always try your best', 'if you don't try you will never succeed' or 'the only thing that matters is winning – there are no prizes for coming second.' Alternatively you may have the economic drive to sustain or improve your standard of living or to meet increasing financial commitments. For some people the opportunity to move into a managerial role coincides with a change in lifestyle, such as buying a home, getting married, having children, and the need to earn enough money to meet new commitments can be very strong. Or the pressure may simply be to get away from a sense of being 'stuck' in your current position. You may have reached the top of the professional grades or pay scales, and need to move into another bracket to improve your prospects.

To live up to your own or other people's expectations of you

A lack of respect for, or belief in, the capabilities of other people can also create a pressure to do something. For example, if you do not have much faith in the ability of your current manager and believe that you could do her/his job just as well (or better), or if you have been told that you are doing so well in your current job that you could easily do the next one 'up the ladder'. Alternatively, you may feel that if you do not apply for the management position someone else will, and you would be less than happy working for that individual. You may even apply for the job in reaction to a casual challenge thrown down such as 'Surely you'll go for it, won't you?'

To protect the people you work with, the unit that you work in or the services you provide

Sometimes the pressure to move into management comes from a sense of frustration, the feeling that the people currently managing the organization do not understand or care enough about the contribution that you and your colleagues provide, and that it will need one of you in a management role to protect those efforts or services. In many organizations there is a strong sense that managers become removed from the front line or 'the real world', and that as a consequence, they do not make decisions in the best interests of the customers or patients, or that they do not take into account professional values in the way that they manage. What may follow these concerns is a pressure to apply for a management post in order to influence the organization in favour of the things you believe in.

The pressures listed so far seem to focus on negative motivation – 'I should' or 'I have to' make the change – but there are a range of positive motivators as well which may include the following:

ILLUSTRATIONS

- 'The opportunity to influence what happens (for good results).'
- 'I have standards that I want to have wider acceptance.'
- 'I enjoy making things happen.'
- 'To share my experience and help others to progress.'
- 'To broaden my horizons – be able to influence for positive change.'
- 'To make things happen more quickly.'
- 'To get more autonomy/responsibility – the freedom to do more of what I want to.'
- 'To get the buzz from achieving visible results.'

A desire to influence the organization to achieve results

If you have strong views about what can be achieved in your organization, you may want to play a part in making it happen. Alternatively, you may have an enthusiasm for the work you do and want to take more responsibility, or a leading role, in achieving the results that you believe are possible (for example, in implementing a new initiative).

A desire to help others to develop their skills

Pride in the knowledge, skills and experience that you have developed may lead to wanting to share them with colleagues, enabling and supporting other people to develop.

Why does it feel like being in a swamp?

In order to explore this issue we would like to use some of the basic concepts of role theory. This approach identifies that the way a person interprets their role largely depends on the expectations that other people have of her/him in that role. The key people you come into contact with in fulfilling a role will have the strongest impact on you. So as a manager, the expectations your staff, colleagues, senior managers and 'customers' have of you will be most important, and these may vary from group to group and organization to organization. It may be clear *what* results you are expected to achieve but not *how* to achieve them (for example, senior management may be more interested in outputs than methods). At the same time, the expectations of these key people may be different and may even be in conflict. Staff may want you to support them and represent their views to more senior managers, while those senior managers may see you as key to influencing your staff to carry through management initiatives. Expectations of you may not be made explicit or may be ambiguous. They may be dependent on your predecessor. If you are expected to behave just like her/him ('all managers are . . . ') or you are expected to work in a completely different way ('a new broom sweeping clean'), this may not fit with how you want to work. There may be simply too many demands made of you in your role, which has been called 'role overload', or people may challenge the legitimacy of the role. In some organizations a major part of the workplace culture is the blaming of management for all problems. If you have joined in that activity in the past it can be difficult to adjust to being one of 'them'.

ILLUSTRATION

A newly appointed manager, 'One of the problems with becoming a manager is that you can't blame "them" any more.'

For all these reasons, people who have moved into management from a professional role often feel much less certain about what their staff expect of them and how they should behave, than they did in their professional role. This is particularly true if staff take the opportunity of having a new manager to challenge his/her authority.

ILLUSTRATION

A Health Service manager, 'You can only be a successful manager if people let you.'

In addition, public image and/or social norms will also play an important part in how you feel about your role, and the public image of managers is less clear and less positive compared to the image of other professions. Managers are not usually 'valued' as much as other professions – for example, doctors – and there are even fewer positive role models –

The swamp metaphor

We have developed the swamp metaphor from working with managers in both public and private sector organizations because many of them seem to share the same strong sense of 'not being in control'. Whether you are producing or distributing goods or delivering services, it seems that a previous sense of stability and certainty is no longer there. The resources available to manage with are constantly shrinking, the requirement for products/services are changing, the demands made on your time are constantly growing, and it often feels impossible to manage the present, let alone plan realistically for the future.

Irritators and challenges are all around. The irritators (flies and mosquitoes) include events and people who distract you from your main purpose. The challenges (alligators) range from international competition for manufacturing to compulsory competition for public services; from government economic and social policy to senior management initiatives and decisions; and from increasingly sophisticated technology to changing attitudes and expectations of staff, bosses, customers, suppliers and the public.

Given these developments and pressures, senior managers may feel they have perfectly valid reasons for introducing organizational change. However, those affected by these changes may not perceive them in the same way. For example, Gaius Petronius Arbiter, a Roman general under Nero, wrote:

> We trained hard, but it seemed that every time we were beginning to form up into teams, we would get reorganised. I was to learn in later life that we tend to meet any new situation by reorganising, and a wonderful method it can be for creating the illusion of progress while producing confusion, inefficiency and demoralisation. (Quoted in Armstrong, M., *A Handbook of Personnel Management Practice*, p. 235.)

This feeling clearly has not changed in nearly 2000 years.

ILLUSTRATION

A senior manager, 'I'm tired. Every time I think I have something under control they change the goal posts. There are so many people wanting different things from me – I don't know whether I'm coming or going and I haven't got time to finish anything.'

In order to cross a swamp you also need to be able to swim through the 'watery places', have lifelines to pull you through, or stepping stones to lift you from the 'boggy bits'. In order to be an effective manager you need the relevant skills (*like swimming*), help and support (*stepping stones and lifelines*) to perform well.

Changing your role, like crossing a swamp, will not always be smooth. It is almost inevitable that you will make mistakes (you fall in), there will be set backs (you get stuck), and you will feel discomfort (you get your feet wet) before you feel confident and competent again in the new role (*reaching the new firm ground*).

Are you in the swamp?

Do you sometimes feel like you are in a swamp? Unsure of your footing? Stuck in the mire or with your head barely above water? Not able to see or steer where you are going? Does it feel like you have lost touch with the firm ground, certainty and therefore your confidence? Do there appear to be endless hazards (alligators) conspiring to disable you? Are there distractions (flies and mosquitoes) diverting your attention from what you are trying to achieve? Do you need help such as being able to swim, lifelines to hang on to or stepping stones to stand on to establish a firm footing – at least temporarily? Do you need a clear incentive to push on to the other side or to some other firm ground? That you are not sure what the new firm ground will be like, but it cannot be worse than the swamp?

Do you feel the need for control?

People have very different levels of tolerance for uncertainty and you may be one of the group who is very uncomfortable with the idea of not being 'in control'.

For example, which of the following apply to you:

1. When planning a holiday, would you book months ahead? Have checked your passport, money and other documents well in advance? Sorted out your clothes and the other things you wish to take days before? Or do you go on the spur of the moment? Have no firm plans, but go where the mood takes you? Throw things in a bag at the last minute?
2. At weekends, or in leisure time, do you have a list of things to do? Have a regular routine to always spend your time in a particular way? Or do you wake up in the morning and think 'OK, what shall I do today?'

Questionnaire: Are you in the swamp?

How do the following statements apply to you?	Always	Sometimes	Never
1. It feels like I am constantly juggling fifteen things at once.			
2. Someone outside my control keeps changing the rules.			
3. I don't know what my staff are doing any more.			
4. Everyone else is talking a different language.			
5. Performance is all about quantity not quality.			
6. I have no time to finish anything.			
7. Everything seems urgent/ a priority.			
8. Everyone expects me to react to their problem now.			
9. There are not enough hours in the day.			
10. I don't know how to handle a difficult member of staff.			
11. Everyone is criticizing me.			

How do the following statements apply to you?	Always	Sometimes	Never
12. I do not have the support of my boss.			
13. I have no time for reflection.			
14. The emphasis is on solving problems immediately.			
15. There is no fun/excitement in my workplace.			
16. Meeting short-term goals is the main criteria of good performance.			
17. I find it difficult to switch off after work.			
18. I am overloaded with unwanted management responsibilities.			
19. I seem to have lost the ability to relax.			
20. My work problems are affecting my private life.			

Scoring
Add 2 points for every 'always'
Add 1 point for every 'sometimes'
Add 0 points for every 'never'

Total score ....

If you have more than 20 points you are definitely in the swamp
Between 10 and 20 then you probably feel like one foot in the swamp
Below 10 and you are on the firm ground

3.   How would you respond to an unexpected invitation to go away this weekend? Would you focus on the problems of re-arranging what you expected to do OR would you jump at the chance?

The higher your need for control, the less comfortable you might be with the unknown or unexpected and the more likely it is that you could feel like you are in a swamp when moving into a managerial role, where in many instances, it is far less obvious what you should do. You may have clear goals or results to aim for, but how to achieve them is less clear.

How would you feel in the swamp?

If you feel very uncomfortable, what options have you got? Do you have the choice of going back into a situation with more certainty? What would make your current situation more certain, or what alternatives are there to move on to another, more acceptable situation? What is clear is that *you* will need to take the initiative – it is not something that other people can do for you. You will need to 'let go' of some things you value, and if you are not to get stuck in the swamp, you need to find new things to replace what has been lost.

Chapter 3

Letting go of the firm ground

No gain without pain. (BENJAMIN FRANKLIN 1706–90)

Introduction

How might it feel to let go of your professional role?

The following are just some of the comments about how individuals have felt about moving out of their professional role:

- 'I felt totally de-skilled.'
- 'It felt like I was stripped naked.'
- 'You don't belong to the club any more.'
- 'You get out of touch so quickly.'
- 'I miss the contact with patients.'
- 'I'd prefer to be on the (drawing) board.'

For many people the profession that they belong to gives them much more than the work that they do, so changing role means losing a great deal.

What do you get from a professional role?

Knowing what you're doing

We have already talked about the route to membership of a professional body requiring a substantial personal investment. The education, training, projects and supervised work, examinations and continuous development required build competence which in turn provides a real sense of the 'firm ground'. People have said that the confidence that comes from such competence is also linked to the feeling of being in control of what you are doing and the decisions that you make.

Enjoyment and a sense of achievement

For many people their profession also means doing the kind of work that they enjoy, for example, helping an elderly person gain mobility after an accident, designing and constructing a bridge or building, teaching children to read or write, and so forth. In many cases there is a real sense of achievement in attending to the detail of the work and immense satisfaction in knowing you are applying all your learning and experience in order to achieve something you believe is worthwhile. Something that you can do and others cannot.

Tangible results/feedback

Equally important to many professionals is the sense of achievement they get from being able to see the tangible results of their work. You can travel on a road you have designed, see a set of accounts, visit a building, talk to a recovered patient, read a pupil's examination results, etc. You can get direct, personal feedback from 'customers', and whether they are satisfied or not, at least this feedback is an indicator of how well you are doing in your work.

Clear guidelines and frameworks within which to work

Professionals also work within clear guidelines and codes of professional practice, with access to more experienced colleagues for advice and guidance. There may be specified methods of working which enable you to be clear about what is expected of you. Sometimes this can feel restrictive, but it also offers security about 'the right way to do things'. You will frequently have more senior colleagues or a manager to offer help or make decisions about the overall resourcing and direction of your work and the organization. This leaves you to get on with your job.

A sense of belonging to a community with shared values

Membership of professional bodies is not conferred lightly. Most professional institutes require not only the demonstration of capability in a particular field, but also personal conformance to standards of behaviour and commitment to ethical codes. Once you belong to 'the club' there is an additional sense of security. Many professional bodies offer direct advice and support to their community of members. They share information using magazines, newsletters, training sessions, meeting forums, and so forth. They also have disciplinary procedures for those who breach the rules so you 'know where you stand'.

Status and recognition as an expert

Belonging to a professional group carries wider recognition than in the workplace. Recognition for the level of commitment, academic ability and the quality of services offered means that many professions have enjoyed the respect of, and deference from, the general public for many years. In the past advice and judgements from these professions were rarely challenged. Although this may now be changing (for example, people are more prepared to challenge their doctor than they would have been ten or twenty years ago) social norms still separate some groups and place them in higher regard than others, valuing their opinions and comments.

Image and social identity

People often say 'I *am* a doctor, social worker, teacher, engineer, scientist' rather than 'I *have* a job in medicine, a school, an engineering company, etc.' The profession that they belong to gives them status in society and an identity which is an important part of their persona.

The ability to blame management

One newly appointed manager told us that the great advantage of being a professional in a large organization was that you could always blame management for the decisions they made, or the problems you were encountering. It was management's responsibility to ensure that there were enough resources to do the job as you want to do it, and so you could expect time out for research, holidays and personal development. This is not always the case in small organizations, but in compensation, in small companies individuals often have more freedom of action.

Control of your own time and work systems

Many professionals, particularly those with senior status, have a considerable amount of freedom in how they organize their time, work load and work systems, and challenges to these have been refuted on the grounds of 'professional integrity' and 'academic freedom'. In the past it has been argued that some organizations have been run 'around' the demands of its senior professionals.

All these factors can contribute to a sense of the 'firm ground'. This includes your competence, confidence, satisfaction, recognition and respect from other people for the expertise that you have. It is not surprising, therefore, that people can find it hard to 'let go'. Social workers may still want to be responsible for certain cases, architects to keep a drawing board, accountants to retain a number of clients and engineers to keep a set of tools and/or equipment.

What motivates you at work?

Difficulty in letting go is even less surprising when you look at the research into motivation at work. Herzberg, Mousiner and Snyderman (1959) is one of many researchers who have developed theories of motivation, and given that his research was conducted with a group of professional engineers, it can be argued to be more relevant to our case than some of the other theories. Herzberg identified that there are a number of factors which affect people's motivation, and therefore performance, at work. He divided them into two categories – those which actively motivated people, which he called motivators, and those which had a negative effect if they were inappropriate or 'wrong' but did not actively enhance performance if they were 'right'. These he called hygiene factors.

Hygiene factors	*Motivators*
• Company policy and administration	• Achievement
• Administration	• Work itself
• Supervision	• Recognition
• Working conditions	• Responsibility
• Status and security	• Advancement
• Interpersonal relationships	• Growth
• Salary	

There was some evidence that salary has an effect both as a hygiene factor and motivator, but in order for it to act as a positive force on someone, there needed to be a perceived direct link between her/his effort and the financial reward.

Comparing this list with what colleagues have said about 'letting go', it would appear that all the things that have actively motivated you about your work are the very things you lose in moving out of a professional role into management. These are as follows:

• Enjoyment of the work itself.
• A sense of achievement from working directly at your profession.
• Feedback and recognition from customers.
• The responsibility that goes with knowing what you are doing.
• The sense of growing/advancing within the profession by the achievement of qualifications and acceptance into the professional association.

As well as a sense of legitimacy from belonging to a professional association.

Furthermore, if you look at the hygiene factors, they may also have a negative effect on you when you become a manager. For example, for a newly appointed manager there is often a lack of the supervision and help that would be available in other jobs. There may also be a lack of status and recognition for you as a junior/middle manager compared with your professional standing. There may be poor working conditions and difficult interpersonal relationships caused by staff who challenge your authority or expertise. All of which suggest that for many people moving into a management role can be very de-motivating and demoralizing.

ILLUSTRATION

From an officer in a public service taking on managerial responsibility for an inner-city office, 'Nobody told me about dealing with the rats, time sheets, petty cash, heating problems, not to mention threats to our personal safety.'

In moving into senior management these things may change significantly. There is usually considerable status and recognition for those at the very top of an organization, together with more attractive terms and conditions of employment and substantial financial rewards. This, however, is only achievable by relatively few people. Many managers feel that they get neither the financial rewards nor the old motivators from their new roles.

So why change?

Why make the transition from professional to manager if it means losing the very things that motivate you, and if, as we suggested in Chapter 1, there appears to be very little security and stability for managers in the current and foreseeable future? We believe the key to being positive about a management role lies in finding new things to value, and in particular in being able to identify tangible measures of success rather than in being demoralized because you are unable to see the results of your efforts and therefore you have no sense of achievement. There is a Swahili proverb that says 'Before a man gives up his old Gods, he should have something of value to replace them.'

The managers we asked about their change in role did see a number of benefits, even if they were initially reluctant to make the change. These benefits included the following:

ILLUSTRATIONS

- 'It's more interesting, you have different horizons.'
- 'It's great to see staff develop and move on.'
- 'I like being able to make a *real* difference.'
- 'Seeing the new unit up and running – and knowing *I did that*.'
- 'The pay and status – eventually.'
- 'Managing my own time, and although I work longer hours, not having to clock in.'
- 'When a member of staff says I have really developed, and that is thanks to you.'
- 'The opportunity to influence what happens (for good results).'
- 'I have standards and I want them to have wider acceptance.'
- 'I enjoy making things happen.'
- 'Being able to share my experience and help others to progress.'
- 'To broaden my horizons and be able to influence for positive change.'
- 'Being able to make things happen more quickly.'
- 'I have more autonomy/responsibility, the freedom to do more of what I wanted to.'

What are the benefits of taking on a managerial role?

A broader view and level of influence

Many people have said that what they really enjoy about being a manager is having a broader view of events, 'being in the know' of what is going on and having access to the political workings of the organization. As a professional, you may believe you have the 'right' answer to a problem or situation, but it can be very frustrating when your ideas do not get taken up. With a wider managerial perspective, you realize that decisions are rarely made based solely on the facts.

Understanding how the organization really works is not only fascinating, but gives you a better opportunity to influence decisions.

The ability to develop your role/service/staff

Because it is possible to understand how decisions are made, it may be easier to influence those decisions in favour of your own part of the organization. You can represent your staff, colleagues and area of work at a higher level, influence systems and key colleagues in order to maximize the opportunities for your staff and the contribution they can make to the organization as a whole.

Personal challenge/growth

Taking on a new role can be seen as a great challenge, and some people enjoy being stretched, taking on what seems impossible and then proving that they can do it. Almost everyone in our research has said that while they may have felt uncomfortable at times, they had actually learned a great deal from becoming a manager. A number of people said that they had become very good at solving problems or 'fielding difficulties', and had gained a great deal of satisfaction from pushing themselves to achieve something which at first seemed beyond them. Reaching targets that once seemed impossible had done wonders for their self-esteem.

Pride in something well done

Other people said they had a real sense of pride in taking responsibility for a department or project and seeing it succeed, and in being able to see the project completed, knowing that you had a major role to play in making it happen, especially if there were measurable results. This might mean taking on additional responsibility for a period of time, but in recompense there is great satisfaction in being able to say ' I did that' or 'without me that project would not have been completed.'

Positive feedback from staff

Praise from staff that they have learned a lot from you, or have valued the way you have managed them, can be very satisfying. It may feel even better to receive positive feedback about your department from more senior managers. Someone described this as 'like the warm glow the whole family gets from reading a good school report for one of your children.'

Taking pleasure from other's success

Taking this a step further a number of managers said that they get a real 'buzz' from helping their staff to develop their potential. When the staff they had managed and coached achieved success, passed exams, or gained a promotion or a new job, they felt that they had contributed to the success and were pleased and proud for the other person.

Controlling your own time

Many managers in the middle levels of organizations are not as much in control of their own time and activities as they may wish to be, and frequently complain about the amount of time they spend in meetings or at the beck and call of others. Nevertheless, they usually have much more opportunity to make decisions about their hours of work and how they spend their time. Work routines are more personalized and flexible than for staff lower in the hierarchy and many people thrive on the variety and pace of work. As one manager said, 'You never have time to get bored and you never know what's coming along next.'

Status and salary – eventually

In the short term moving from professional to manager may involve losing a sense of status and may not mean a higher salary (in real terms). However, in climbing the ladder, the rewards for senior managers become more significant and tangible. As well as an increased salary, these may include a variety of benefits, such as a car, private health care, pension contributions, more holidays, profit sharing, and so forth. In fact, at the time of writing, the rewards to senior executives in some organizations are so very high compared to the rest of their staff that they are triggering the demand for upper limits to be set.

Which of these benefits as discussed above can you identify with? Which ones would have a positive effect on you, encouraging you to let go of your professional firm ground and cross the swamp? How will you do it? In order to take the journey you first need to be prepared to try new things. How willing are you to '*test the water*'?

Questionnaire: Letting go

1. Are you hanging on to the past? Which of the following features of a professional role would you value most?

    • Knowing what you're doing.
    • Enjoyment and a sense of achievement.
    • Tangible results/feedback.
    • Clear guidelines and frameworks within which to work.
    • A sense of belonging to a community with shared values.
    • Status and recognition as an expert.
    • Image and social identity.
    • The ability to blame management.
    • Control of your own time and work systems.
    • Other?

2. What have you let go of?
    •
    •
    •
    •

3. Which of the following benefits would you (or do you) value in the management role?
    • A broader view and level of influence.
    • The ability to develop your role/service/staff.
    • Personal challenge/growth.
    • Pride in something well done.
    • Positive feedback from staff.
    • Taking pleasure from other's success.
    • Controlling your own time.
    • Status and salary – eventually.

Are they sufficient for you to enjoy being a manager?

4. What do you still need to do? List below the key features of your professional role, the key features of your current or potential management role as you see them. Then, identify those things that you currently continue to do, that you should stop doing; and those things that you currently do not do, that you should develop as part of your management role. At the same time identify how to build in those benefits which you would value most.

Professional role	Management role	Stop doing	Start doing	Develop benefits

Chapter 4

Testing the water

No one knows what he can do until he tries.

(PUBLILIUS SYRUR, c. 442 BC)

Introduction

Imagine you have been asked if you are interested in taking on a new three-year project. It would represent a development of your career and while it is something you could do, you would need to put in a lot of time to bring yourself up to date with the work so far. In addition, you would need to learn a new computer system and another language because the project will be based in another country. It will also mean moving the family. Your partner works and you have one child in her second year at school.

How would you feel about such a change?

Changing from professional to manager

Your attitude and approach to making the transition from professional to manager will depend on a number of factors. Like many other situations a key factor will be your willingness to make the change. If it is your decision and you want to be a manager, then you will probably be excited. You may feel apprehensive, but it is unlikely you would also be resistant. On the other hand, if the move into management has been imposed by someone else, or you are making it because it seems like there is no alternative, then you are likely to feel much more negative and reluctant.

Figure 4.1 is based in the premiss that when people are faced with fundamental unexpected or unwanted changes they tend to go through a series of stages. The first stage represents the current situation which is accepted and is the *status quo*. The second stage is usually *denial* – refusing to admit the change is really taking place or that they will really be

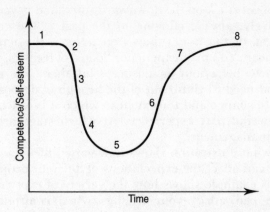

Notes: 1 status quo; 2 denial; 3 minimization; 4 depression; 5 acceptance;
6 testing new behaviour; 7 making sense; 8 new status quo

Figure 4.1 The stages in change

affected by it. In extreme situations of physical shock or trauma the person may never move from this state, but blank out the situation completely from their memory. Denial is followed by *minimization*. This is characterized by a person playing down the significance of the change or its effect on her/him, until the realization occurs that the change is not only real, but will also have a significant effect on her/him. People then move into the next phase, which is *depression*. In this stage individuals may become very 'flat', unable to find energy or enthusiasm for anything at all. They use expressions like 'What's the point?'

Throughout these phases people are looking backwards, clinging to the past, unable to see, or refusing to acknowledge, anything positive in the change as their morale and self-esteem fall. It is not until the point at which the situation is faced and *accepted* that people can let go of the past and start to look to the future. Their morale begins to recover and they will try new ways of coping with the situation – *testing new behaviours*. If these activities are successful then the person will rapidly recover her/his self-esteem and morale, and improve her/his performance; if they are not, the person will fall back into depression and want things to be as they were in the past.

The next phase involves trying to *make sense of the change*. If this is possible and has a positive impact, then the new situation becomes accepted as the *new status quo* and the individual will feel fine until the next unwanted change when the cycle may begin again.

The length of time that this process of transition takes and the depth of depression will vary from person to person depending on both the nature of the change and her/his attitude to it. In extreme cases an individual can get stuck on the downward spiral and never face up to the change positively, always clinging to the past – 'the good old days', 'what I do best' or the 'way things were'. Nor is the actual experience necessarily linear. You may experience 'loops' of feelings, for example, if testing out new behaviour is unsuccessful then you may revert to depression and need to climb out of the 'trough of despondency' again. Adaptability to change and the extent to which it is welcomed may also depend on specific past experience. At which stage are you in your transition to management?

The following illustration shows how varied life experiences can be and how that can affect the expectations of different people in the same situation. This example shows how the variety of experiences through-out your life can affect your feelings when confronted with new situations. It also suggests that you can have very different attitudes to learning which will have been developed as the result of various factors. These would include how varied your previous life experiences have been and how you felt about them.

ILLUSTRATION

At the beginning of a three-day residential course we asked everyone to share their feelings and expectations about the programme. Sandra and Peter were two of the participants.

Peter was extremely apprehensive, unsure what to expect, uncomfortable at sleeping in a strange place, concerned at what he might be asked to do and afraid of making a fool of himself. He felt some resentment at being put in the position of feeling obliged to attend and was not sure he would learn anything useful. He said:

> I was born and brought up in a small town near here, and have always lived in the same house I was born in. I went to two local schools before attending the local college and then started work for a company in the next town, getting my qualifications at the college by day release from my employer. I've enjoyed my job as a maintenance engineer, but this last year the boss has wanted me to take on some managerial responsibility – and so has sent me on this residential course. I've never been away from home without my wife in all the years we've been married and I did not want to come. But the boss said it was expected, so in the end I agreed.

Sandra was on the same course. She was also concerned about making a fool of herself, but she had some idea what to expect, was quite used to staying in different places and was confident she would learn a lot. She said:

> As a child my parents moved house fairly regularly, so I attended six different schools and three universities in various

> parts of the country. Since getting married I have lived in five
> places, including three years in another country. My first job
> involved visiting a number of companies in a wide
> geographical area, the second was teaching in a college and
> the third working in a central department in a large local
> authority. I have attended other management training courses
> in the past and so was quite keen to come on this one.

Attitudes to learning

This will not only depend on the range of experience(s) you have had of learning but also how enjoyable (or uncomfortable) they have been.

How many people do you know who do not like or 'cannot' learn a particular subject because of a bad experience at school or college? Being ridiculed or punished for failing to achieve can create a very strong block to learning.

Equally, if most of your experience has been limited to formal, structured, 'taught' programmes, then that will condition your expectations, and different approaches would probably make you feel very uncomfortable. If you learnt well from this type of programme, then you would probably want to repeat it. On the other hand, if you found learning difficult or not enjoyable then, understandably, you would probably be reluctant to go through those feelings again.

How willing are you to learn?

Some people seem to go through life always curious, interested, willing to try new things; others prefer the comfort of the known, 'tried and tested' ways of working. Which are you?

There are lots of well-known phrases used when people are resisting a change. The following are some of the most common excuses we have heard:

- 'We tried it before and it didn't work then.'
- 'Ah yes . . . but we're different.'
- 'We've always done it this way.'
- 'It's not my responsibility.'
- 'The unions will never go along with it.'
- 'It's not company policy.'
- 'We don't have the authority.'
- 'You're right but . . .'

- 'We need a working party.'
- 'You can't teach an "old dog" new tricks.'
- 'It might be OK in your organization . . . but it can't be done here.'
- 'We don't have enough resources.'
- 'We haven't got the time.'
- 'It will never happen here.'
- 'I'm too old for all this.'
- 'But I have got "nn" years experience in this job.'

How often do you hear yourself saying this sort of thing?

How do we learn?

Young children frequently learn by experimentation and are often encouraged to learn this way by being given toys that they can take apart and then reconstruct. However, these toys also encourage the child to think about what s/he is doing, to learn from experience and not to make the same mistakes more than once. After a certain age, children will also develop a more 'conceptual' approach to learning. These are the times when they seem to constantly ask questions to make sense of the world, such as: How does this work? Why did he say that? What does this animal eat? How do these people live? Why is the sky blue? Where does rain come from? Gradually they develop the ability to make connections between the different things that they learn and transfer learning from one situation to another.

According to David Kolb (1984) this process of learning also applies to adults. He argues that effective learning takes place in a four-stage cycle: the first stage is concrete *experience* – or learning by doing; the second is *reflection* – or taking time out to think about the experience; the third is to *make sense of the learning* by applying a *theory* or framework to it; and the fourth is to consider how to *apply the learning in a practical way* – how to adapt what has been learnt to other situations. These four stages are illustrated in Figure 4.2.

Research has shown, however, that although we need to be capable of learning in all four stages, we each develop preferences for one or more of the four styles as shown in Figure 4.3. How we want to learn is often linked to the success or failure, comfort or discomfort, we have experienced in previous situations. Building on the learning cycle then, we can look at personal preferences. People who learn best from experience are called *activists*, those who find it more effective to have time out to think are called *reflectors*, those who prefer a framework are called *theorists* and those who want to focus on putting the learning into practice are seen as *pragmatists*.

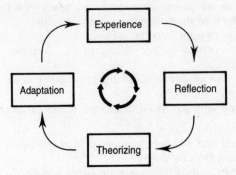

Figure 4.2   The learning cycle

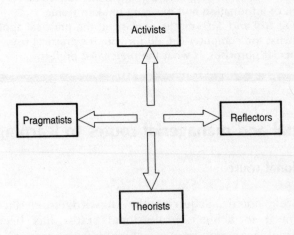

Figure 4.3   Four learning styles

How do you prefer to learn?

1.   Imagine you have just bought a new personal computer. What is the first thing you would do?
  (a)   Take it out of the box, plug it in and start 'playing'.
  (b)   Think about how you have used one in the past and what this one might do if you press certain keys and functions.
  (c)   Read the manual (or anything else which explains how computers work) carefully before doing anything.
  (d)   Talk to a friend/expert about what practical use you will make of it and focus on setting it up specifically for those purposes.

2. Imagine you are going swimming in a place you have never been before. Which of the following would you do?
    (a) Plunge straight into the water.
    (b) Watch others before going in, to find the best place and approach.
    (c) Find out all about local tides, weather conditions and local customs.
    (d) Decide why you want to swim – either for exercise or for fun.

If you chose 1(a) and 2(a) then you are probably an *activist* one of those people who learn best by doing.
If you chose 1(b) and 2(b) you are probably a *reflector*, someone who prefers to think about experiences and learn from them.
Choosing 1(c) and 2(c) implies you are a *theorist*, someone who has a preference for understanding the theory behind something, such as how the computer works, by studying the manual or textbooks; or researching the conditions for swimming before going in the water. You tend to want a framework of information and meaning to learn from.
In choosing 1(d) and 2(d), that is, looking at the practical application of learning (what the computer can do for you, it's practical use, swimming for a particular purpose), is what the *pragmatist* prefers.

Professional and managerial routes to learning

The professional route

For many professionals, acquiring the knowledge and developing the skills they need to achieve professional status has been done by attending formal 'academic' courses which in most cases are defined and structured by the appropriate professional body and assessed by formal examinations. The programmes may be based on full-time study or part-time courses while also doing a job. In either case, they may include some applied 'project work', which would be completed under supervision from a more senior person in the profession. In addition, there are usually clear models, frameworks and theories to work with, and you would be expected to be able to apply them in a number of situations. Many professions also now require 'continuous professional development' which is also frequently based on attending courses.

This approach would suggest that the least used learning style is that of the activist. In developing your professional skills there may be times when you do learn by 'jumping in the deep end' but it would not be the norm.

The management route

There is now a wide range of management education and training courses available to most people. However, despite a considerable increase in both qualification-based and shorter management courses, and in contrast to professionals many people still find themselves in the management role with very little, if any, real preparation for it. These managers need to learn from their own experience which is the opposite to the pattern of learning for professionals.

For those managers who do have the opportunity to attend a training programme, the organizers often expect, even require, a minimum length of experience as a manager before attending. Even in organizations with well-developed and run 'management trainee programmes' the relevance and timing of courses are often cause for concern for participants.

ILLUSTRATIONS

- 'Yes I had the chance to attend a management course, but not until I had been doing the job for nearly a year.'
- 'The problem is that courses don't cover the real problems you have to deal with day to day.'
- 'Well I'm sure looking at appraisal skills will be very interesting but I don't actually supervise anyone at the moment – and am not likely to for at least another year.'
- 'We've just spent the whole session (three hours) racing through different management theories – so what!'

While some management programmes are structured and knowledge based like professional courses, there are many more which are 'experiential'. That is, they are designed to enable participants to learn by undertaking different activities (be activists) and then analyzing their experiences (reflecting) and drawing conclusions from them to apply in their workplace (adapting). The model is often described as 'plan – do – review' and is argued to be more effective because it more accurately reflects the situation that managers actually work in. The underlying assumption is that much of managerial activity is skills based, and like a sport or other similar activities 'practice makes perfect'. At the same time, if there is no single clear definition of management, and measures of effectiveness vary from organization to organization, individuals will need to learn from their own experience to be their own judge of what makes them effective (or not).

Having had experience, however, does not necessarily mean that someone has learned from it. (Have you heard the question, 'Have you really had x years of experience or one year x times over?') The opportunity to learn from experience is always there, but the question is: How willing are you to use it? As Peter Honey, the management writer, said, ' Learning from experience is too important to be left to chance.'

What are the issues for 'older' learners?

However, having completed a number of years of study, project work and supervized activity to gain a professional qualification, many people reach a point where they have 'had enough'. This often coincides with changes in personal circumstances and increased domestic commitments which add to the feeling of wanting to consolidate rather than take on further learning.

Research has also shown that as we get older it is more difficult to sustain enthusiasm, energy and a focus for learning. Learning, therefore, can be seen more as a threat than an opportunity, and attending a course seen as a judgement of failure or that past experience is no longer valued. Fear of being embarrassed by younger 'whiz kids' or of 'making a fool of yourself' can create real resistance to learning.

For other people it is simply complacency – to learn something new means they will be expected to do something about it and they do not want to exert themselves. They cannot 'be bothered'.

Unfortunately this stage in your life also frequently coincides with the opportunity to move into a management role, the need to learn new skills and to undertake that learning in a different context.

Taking responsibility for your own learning

If organizational opportunities to develop your managerial skills are somewhat haphazard it suggests that you need to take the initiative by taking responsibility for your own development. In moving into a new role the problem is that sometimes 'you don't know what you don't know'. This problem has been described by the following four stages in Figure 4.4. The fact that 'you don't know what you don't know' could be described as the first stage or *'unconscious incompetence'*. Think about learning to drive a car. If you have no experience at all, have never thought about learning or have never even watched someone else driving, then you don't know what has to be learned. However, by having watched someone else drive or taken a first lesson, you may become very aware of what has to be done even though you cannot yet do it. That is *'conscious incompetence'*. *'Conscious competence'* is the point at which you can drive but have to think about everything, consciously

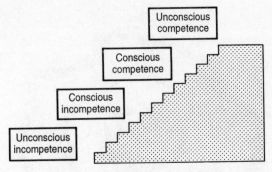

Figure 4.4 The learning process

while '*unconscious competence*' would describe the mind state of highly experienced drivers. This does not imply that these drivers are not thinking or alert to what is going on around them, but the co-ordination of steering, changing gear, braking, looking ahead and checking in rear-view mirrors are all things that are done 'automatically'. In developing any skill there is a difference between knowing what should be done and being able to repeat a standard of behaviour on a regular basis – being competent.

Managing the transition to management

A key feature of making the transition to management successfully, therefore, is being able to review your own willingness to change and being prepared to let go of your professional 'firm ground' and step into what may be a swamp.

Because there are many different approaches to management training and development, it will help enormously if you are able to assess your own preferences in learning styles and choose which approach will be more effective for you as an individual. See the chapters on stepping stones and lifelines to explore the help you may want.

In making the change you will need to develop new skills and approaches, and demonstrate competence in a variety of circumstances where different measures of that competence may exist. Learning to 'learn from experience' will be a key factor in your success. You may need to actively look for those opportunities you can learn from, which may mean taking risks or being prepared occasionally to 'make a fool of yourself', particularly in the 'safe' environment of a training course. As someone said to us recently, 'You cannot cross a swamp without getting your feet dirty or occasionally falling over.' What would make it

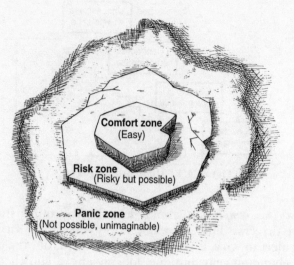

Figure 4.5   Testing the water

worthwhile for you? The following are some of the benefits that people have identified for being open to learning:

- 'It will make life easier (I want to reduce the hassle).'
- 'It will be more interesting/enjoyable (I want to learn).'
- 'I will be proud of myself if I achieve this.'
- 'Someone else will be proud of me (whose opinion matters).'
- 'I will have improved my prospects.'
- 'I believe in what I am doing.'
- 'I like a challenge.'
- 'There is a (cash) incentive to do something new.'
- 'I will be in trouble if I do not learn this.'
- 'It is a stepping stone to something more attractive.'

How often do you hear yourself saying this sort of thing?

Activity: Testing the water

PART 1   Think about your current abilities and limits. Things that you would consider easy or have no qualms about would fit into your comfort zone as illustrated in the centre of Figure 4.5. Those things which you would find more difficult or risky but feel you could accomplish belong in the risk zone. Those things you would find impossible or unimaginable should be located in the outer ring or panic zone.

Use the following list to trigger the exercise, but add as many items of your own as you wish.

1.   Make a presentation on management theory.
2.   Tell a musician or actor how much you have just enjoyed their performance.
3.   Go to live in another country for a number of years.
4.   Take up wood carving.
5.   Write a book and submit it to a publisher.
6.   Go on a strict diet – and stick to it.
7.   Eat baby octopus in a Mediterranean restaurant.
8.   Take the lead in an amateur play.
9.   Go down a coal mine.
10. Learn a new physical skill (e.g. skiing, swimming or rock climbing).
11. Make a parachute jump.
12. Sing in a Karaoke bar.
13. Go to a student night-club.
14. Lead an expedition of young people to the mountains.
15. Keep a detailed set of financial accounts for a year.
16. Cry in front of your friends.
17. Take your pet to stay in a high class hotel.
18. Say no to your boss.
19. Confront someone smoking in a non-smoking compartment on the train.
20. Learn a new computer system.
21.
22.
23.
24.
25.

PART 2   Look at the picture you have created and see if there are any patterns to the things you find risky or impossible (e.g. such as fear for your physical safety or fear of public ridicule).

PART 3   Refer back to your preferred learning style and use your preference to plan two new activities to try. One which will enhance your personal abilities and the other which will develop a useful workplace skill.

Action 1

Action 2

Chapter 5

Swimming

Like a trap set for a mouse, the system (in our schools, families and organizations) is rigged to catch people's weaknesses rather than build on their strengths. (CLIFTON AND NELSON 1992)

Introduction

In Chapter 3 we listed a number of quotes from people who said that they had experienced a sense of being 'de-skilled' when making the transition from a professional to a manager. It is natural that any change in your job is likely to bring new activities and therefore the need for new skills. As a manager, some of these new activities might include being responsible for drawing up or managing a budget, or offering leadership and support to others, but an additional problem for many managers comes from being responsible for 'achieving results through people' rather than by their own efforts. If those people (your staff) question your actions and judgements much more than previous 'customers' would have done, such challenges can make you feel doubly unsure of your abilities.

In *Play to Your Strengths*, Clifton and Nelson (1992) identify that, in an attempt to encourage learning across all fields of ability, individuals and organizations seem to focus much more readily on someone's weaknesses than on their strengths. Parents will encourage their children to be 'good all rounders' or might encourage them to be good in the things that the parents themselves value. Similarly, organizations will attempt to fit employees into ready-made niches rather than identify and play to their individual strengths. Yet how much more energy could be generated if we focused on people's strengths and sought to manage or minimize their weaknesses, rather than focus on their limitations and 'let the strengths take care of themselves'?

What are the transferable skills?

It is clear that many skills developed during professional training and practice are equally appropriate to managers. For example, people from a technical background, such as engineers, scientists, building surveyors and medical personnel, should have well-developed analytical and problem-solving skills, while individuals from the 'people-based' occupations, such as social work, nursing, training and education, should bring highly developed interpersonal and action planning skills. In addition, in many professions it is widely expected that senior professionals will actively supervise students or newly appointed staff during a probationary period. Is this something you are good at? Can it be easily transferred into your management role?

ILLUSTRATIONS

From a nurse manager, 'I use the same problem-solving framework as a manager as I used to analyze background, diagnose, treat and discharge patients.'

From an engineer, 'I'm used to solving technical problems, I just have to use the same approach for organizational ones.'

View of the managerial role

Frequently, the problem in changing roles lies in identifying what skills you are currently using and being able to apply the same skills in a different context. Changing roles has been described as 'learning to look at the world through a different window', in which the new view may initially seem quite strange, but once you have got used to a new perspective, you may see many similarities.

Almost every professional will need to do the following:

- Ask questions and listen to the answers.
- Collect information to help make decisions and solve problems.

As a professional you may already be familiar with the problem-solving process model as illustrated in Figure 5.1. The same approach also applies for managers. The type of information may be different, the problem unusual and the decision more complex, but the basic process is the same. It has been our experience that part of the problem in transferring skills is the assumptions that are made about the new role. It is concerning how many people, when in their management role,

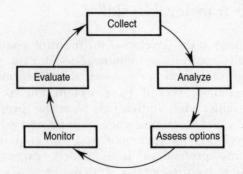

Figure 5.1   The problem-solving process

forget to ask questions but simply pass judgement on a situation without collecting all the facts. They do not really listen to what is being said because they have already made up their mind.

Do you remember the myth that 'managers must have all the answers'? There is something about general perceptions about a particular role. Just as a teacher can frequently be heard using such leading questions with children as 'That was a stupid thing to do wasn't it?' or 'You weren't thinking were you ?' where the child is really only expected to agree with what is being said; similarly, when someone becomes a manager they frequently use leading questions to confirm her/his opinion rather than collect information. Intellectually, they would argue that asking open and probing questions will not only lead to better informed decisions, but can also build empathy with the other person by demonstrating that you are listening to them. However, when actually in the managerial role, they somehow forget how to use this key skill. If you feel uncomfortable with a role, you may lose some of the skills you could readily use in other situations.

In addition, there are many skills that are transferable from the other areas of your life. Do you manage the family budget or coach young people in a sport? Do you organize events or chair meetings for a social club? These skills may be of real value at work too.

Skills are not finite – they can always be improved or practised in a different context. You may have passed your driving test, but does that mean you could enter the RAC rally? You may be able to swim half a kilometre in a heated indoor pool but could you do so in a cold, rough sea? You could learn to. Once you have learned the basics of any skill you can improve your performance by practising and getting feedback. As David Kolb identified, the final stage in the learning cycle is adaptation. This means being able to transfer the learning into different situations. This development process can be illustrated in the following way:

1. *Learning by rote* means that you might be able to do something but would do it in a very mechanical way, or that you can remember and repeat what is learnt, but not necessarily understand or apply the learning, (e.g. a speech from Shakespeare repeated without inflection or meaning, or repeating arithmetic tables).
2. *Applied learning* means you not only have the knowledge but can also put it into practice (e.g. making sense of the speech or using the mental arithmetic when shopping).
3. *Integrated learning* is the third stage when what is learned is fully understood and integrated into the way you see and do things, such as a highly skilled actor 'living the part' or using the arithmetic skills in many areas of your life.

Have you got such well-developed skills that they can easily transfer into your management role?

What are the key skills that managers need?

The answer to the question of the key skills that managers need will depend on the specific requirements of an individual job. There are many different roles that carry the title 'manager'. Not all of them require you to be able to demonstrate the full range of managerial skills. One of your first tasks as a newly appointed manager is to find out exactly what is expected of you, to what standards you must perform and under what circumstances. You will need to identify the following:

*   Those skills that you will need to be a successful manager, and to what extent they can have been learned and developed within your profession.
*   Your level of ability or the level of development of these skills; to what standards.
*   The context in which you will need to use them.

Can you practise these skills just as capably in one situation as another? The list will provide you with an initial assessment of the managerial skills which you already use in your professional or other roles, and their transferability into your management role.

The development of competency models

Since the 1948 Education Act there have been many changes to the education and vocational training frameworks in Britain. Most recently National Vocational Qualifications (NVQs) have been developed as part of a national drive to develop consistent definitions of what is expected of people at work, and to focus education and training programmes on building practical skills and competencies or 'demonstrable capability'. For managers, the Management Charter Initiative (MCI) is the body responsible for developing the standards of competence for managers at three levels – M1-junior management, M2-middle management and M3-senior management. For levels 1 and 2 there are 4 key areas: (i) managing operations (ii) managing finance (iii) managing people and (iv) managing information. Each of which is divided into units and sub-divided into elements of competence. You may wish to use the Chart 5.1 on pp. 60–1 to review how many of these elements you can demonstrate and at what level of learning you can apply them.

However, while the management standards do offer a general framework, they have also highlighted the difficulties in trying to produce a single definition for a series of complex roles across all types of organization. They identify the elements of competence and the range of situations in which they should be demonstrated, but they do not give defined levels of performance. They represent a static model assuming a level of certainty, not taking account of the changing needs of organizations in the future.

A Skills Profile

Which of these management skills do you already practise at work (or in another context)?

Activity/result focused skills	Work	Not work	Transferable
		(Tick as appropriate)	
Setting objectives	......	......	......
Deciding priorities	......	......	......
Planning workload and staff needs	......	......	......
Allocating resources to meet targets	......	......	......
Organizing work	......	......	......
Setting and agreeing work methods	......	......	......
Project planning and managing	......	......	......
Developing and using monitoring systems	......	......	......
Briefing – giving information to staff	......	......	......
Handling disruption to work	......	......	......
Scheduling work to achieve deadlines	......	......	......
Monitoring and reviewing performance	......	......	......

People skills
Questioning and listening   ....
Motivating staff   ....
Presenting proposals   ....
Leading discussion   ....
Chairing meetings   ....
Participating in meetings   ....
Interviewing   ....
Dealing with conflicting demands   ....
Influencing   ....
Building teamwork   ....
Giving feedback   ....
Coaching or training   ....
Counselling   ....

Financial skills
Managing cash flow   ....
Interpreting financial information ....
Developing and managing budgets   ....
Producing financial analysis   ....
Producing trading accounts   ....
Producing profit and loss accounts ....

Information handling skills
Collecting, analyzing/evaluating:
   verbal information   ....
   numerical information ....
   financial information ....
Developing information systems   ....
(including computers)   ....
Using information systems   ....
(including computers)   ....
Preparing and justifying proposals ....
Making decisions   ....
Solving problems   ....

Managing change skills
Assessing potential changes at work   ....
Reviewing current working practices   ....
Gaining commitment to change   ....
Negotiating and agreeing changes   ....
Implementing change   ....

**How many of these management skills have you already got?
What can you do to develop them?**

An alternative approach to competencies

One thing we can be certain about is that in future managers will have both complex and changing roles. Peters and Quinn (1988) point out that our view of what constitutes effective performance will inevitably be dynamic and changing. We need to develop a more flexible framework for managerial competencies and their relevance to the future, and appreciate that the further ahead we look, the less specific our information is, and therefore investment in it will have limited value. It is clear, however, that as an organization moves through different business environments, or itself matures, or as your management role changes and evolves then the relevance of any one competency is bound to alter.

The following perspective, developed by Sparrow and Boam (1992), balances the notion of developing competencies for change with the changing role of competencies, by taking a life-cycle perspective which addresses many of the limitations of traditional approaches to competency.

Rather than creating generic lists of competencies that are associated with 'coping with change' or 'making change happen', organizations should develop a more sophisticated picture of competencies at the organizational level by thinking of any particular competency as having a 'life cycle'. The relevance of any competency to an organization (or to a career group or individual job) will wax and wane. Standing in the present and looking out to the future, organizations should expect to see the following four different categories of competency as illustrated in Figure 5.2.

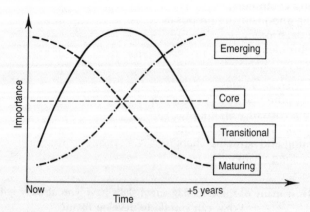

Figure 5.2   Competency life cycles

1. Emerging competencies.
2. Maturing competencies.
3. Transitional competencies.
4. Core competencies.

Emerging competencies

These competencies may not be particularly relevant to the organization and its jobs at present, but given the organization's strategic path they will become more important in the future. For example, a public sector organization facing compulsory competition or privatization could identify that the demands of planned price control regimes, regulated standards of customer service, business diversification, shareholder expectations of increased profitability and the devolution of responsibility within the business would increase the need for senior managers to demonstrate the following:

• More outward looking behaviour.
• Commercial and competitive awareness.
• Anticipation and planning of business change.
• Better utilization of resources.
• A shift away from managing activities to leading people.

To design a management development process and identify fast-track managers capable of performing successfully in this new environment, the organization would have to be able to identify competencies that in no way would be obvious from questioning existing managers.

Maturing competencies

In other cases, some competencies may have played an important part in organizational life (and the jobs within it) in the past, but will become increasingly less relevant in the future. For example, compare the five key competencies for managers identified thirty years ago by a major oil company with its more recent list:

Original list	*Current list*
• 'Helicopter' (strategic) vision.	• 'Helicopter' (strategic) ability.
• Analytical skills.	• Analytical skills.
• Imagination.	• Imagination and creativity.
• A sense of reality.	• A sense of reality and worldliness.

- Leadership.

- Decisiveness divided into;
- – influencing and motivating;
- – effective delegation;
- – ability to communicate;
- – business sense.

Transitional competencies

A third group of competencies is called transitional. Take an organization that wants to identify some senior managers to head up a new
business area as it embarks on a major expansion and acquisition
programme. In the early stages of their new roles these managers will
probably be required to do the following:

- Demonstrate a high capacity to live with uncertainty.
- Manage stress (in themselves and their new colleagues).
- Cope with pressures.
- Manage conflict.

Because these transitional competencies are often seen as negative
and may only be relevant for a short period of time, they may be
overlooked when competencies are being identified. Yet change can only
be achieved or managed smoothly if they are emphasized. They are
transitional, but are also integral to the process of change, so are still
very relevant.

Core competencies

The fourth category of competencies is called stable or core. They
endure and will still be as important tomorrow as they are today. In any
organization there will be competencies that are central to its effective
performance despite the current or future 'flavour' of the business plan
or strategy. Evans (1991) highlights that we are in danger of becoming
obsessed with change, improvement and transformation at the expense
of those competencies needed for continuity and implementation such as
reasoning or analytical ability, which are likely to be core competencies
in almost every setting.

Other core competencies may relate to the way business is carried
out in the particular sector (public, private, industrial or commercial).
In Britain, the management of change in the Health Service has received
a lot of attention, but there are examples where limiting the focus on the

future has led to serious difficulties. For example, a particular Health Authority department was about to undergo a major change, converting to agency status. Competency profiles were established in order to recruit a group of external managers into senior positions. The profile included the expected new focus on communication skills, strategic planning, and so on, but a subsequent comparison to competency work done elsewhere in the Authority showed that in focusing on future priorities, the profile had totally overlooked a number of core competencies that would be critical for new managers. The main competency overlooked, which was of critical importance, was organizational and political sensitivity. The managers who were recruited were in fact very poor in this, and as a result, they failed in their tasks and the high investment in them was wasted. Core competencies provide continuity and they need to be built in, not lost.

Updating your competency profile

In thinking about and classifying your competencies as being stable, emerging, declining or transitional, it becomes easier to understand the idea of a 'shelf life' for a competency profile. Clearly, the importance or weighting that you give to any one competency will change in proportion to the speed of change within your business environment and the nature of the job you do. However, the time and cost invested in classifying your competencies in relation to their life cycle does not need to be onerous. The more forward-looking your profile is, the longer its shelf life will be. The more it is possible to classify competencies, the easier it is to 'update' only those competencies that have a changing emphasis. You need to ask the following questions:

- Are the emerging competencies so relevant that they become a central part of your profile from now on?
- Have the maturing competencies dropped in importance so much that they are no longer worth investing?
- Do you still need to consider the transitional competencies?
- What are the core competencies?

In updating your profile, the first thing is likely to be shifting the 'weighting' given to various competencies, rather than having to re-define them. It is of course impossible to put a finite figure in years and months on any profile. However, it would be reasonable to assume that as a manager you will have to re-identify your competencies once every three years. You may wish to look at the questionnaire at the end of this chapter to think about your own competency profile and how and when to update it.

Adapting to the environment

One of Sparrow and Boam's core competencies is 'organizational and political sensitivity' and yet one of the key problems facing many professionals moving into a management role is their lack of understanding of how decisions get made and implemented in their organizations. As a professional, the way that you analyze information and present it is usually based in the theoretical framework of the profession – recommendations are made using your 'best professional judgement'. For example, engineers will use logical rational argument to present a proposal, whereas teachers may use a model of learning and health carers might present information based on the best interests of the patient. However, decisions in organizations are made for many different reasons. Not getting your recommendations accepted may have little to do with the logic of your argument, but the perspective and interests of the decision makers. If senior management is under enormous pressure to cut the current budget, a recommendation to buy new computers or recruit more staff will not be taken up no matter how well argued the case. You may not have become 'de-skilled' in terms of collecting and analyzing information or even presenting a proposal. It may be more about understanding what will influence the decision makers, who may have other priorities. You may not be able to influence them, and then have to accept the situation as not ideal, or you may be able to develop the skills to understand those priorities and work to them.

What personal attributes do you need?

The following personal attributes are also important:

- Confidence.
- Self-esteem.
- Resilience.
- Persistence.
- Energy/stamina.
- Drive.
- Determination

These characteristics may be harder to specify than the work-based skills previously mentioned, but are just as important to you. They will contribute to your ability to succeed in a different role.

Hersey and Blanchard's model of situational leadership (1988) identifies a concept called 'task maturity'. It suggests that in developing in a job or in performing a particular task, you need both competence and confidence to reach your full potential. People who are task mature not only have the basic knowledge and skills, but they also get the job done. They not only have experience, but they have also learned from that experience and so do not repeat mistakes. They are highly motivated, think through the consequences of their actions and are willing to try new things. They do not take a narrow focus of their work but think about how it fits into a broader picture. They bring both energy and enthusiasm to their work.

As you develop within a professional role you will usually become highly task mature; if you change that role you will (understandably) be less task mature. You may, however, have become used to being successful, to having more junior colleagues seeking your opinion and advice and not needing to seek advice yourself. At the same time the organization may have seen you as highly successful too. People are often promoted into a management role because they are perceived to be very successful in their current position and it is assumed that they can easily transfer to the new role.

In changing roles, you become less task mature and it can be very difficult to ask for help if it is not readily offered to you. There is frequently an expectation that you can 'hit the ground running', which is why you need the personal strengths to make the change successfully.

ILLUSTRATION

When she joined a local authority in 1984, Sheila was already a qualified trainer with ten years experience working with managers and staff in many different organizations, but when drafting a letter after a meeting with a departmental manager she thought 'I will just check it with a colleague,' and was stunned to be told, 'You cannot send the letter in your own name. It has to go out under the signature of the Chief Officer.' She felt totally 'de-skilled' both as a trainer and letter writer. Despite many years experience as a professional there was a new set of rules for behaving as a manager (in that particular organization) which had to be learned. She was never comfortable writing letters in the third person, but had to accept the system was not going to change and learn how to adapt to it.

We explored the stages you go through in dealing with change in a previous chapter. In letting go of your professional role the fourth stage

Chart 5.1 Summary of occupational standards for managers as defined in the

Occupational standards
1.1 Identify opportunities for improvements in services, products and systems **1.2** Evaluate proposed changes for benefits and disadvantages **1.3** Negotiate and agree the introduction of change **1.4** Implement and evaluate changes to services, products and systems **1.5** Introduce, develop and evaluate quality assurance systems
2.1 Establish and maintain the supply of resources into the organization/ department **2.2** Establish and agree customer requirements **2.3** Maintain and improve operations against quality and functional specifications **2.4** Create and maintain the necessary conditions for productive work
3.1 Control costs and enhance value **3.2** Monitor and control activities against budgets
4.1 Justify proposals for expenditure on projects **4.2** Negotiate and agree budgets
5.1 Define future personnel requirements **5.2** Determine specifications to secure quality people **5.3** Assess and select candidates against team and organizational requirements
6.1 Develop and improve teams through planning and activities **6.2** Identify, review and improve development activities for individuals **6.3** Develop oneself within the job role **6.4** Evaluate and improve the development processes used
7.1 Set and update work objectives for teams and individuals **7.2** Plan activities and determine work methods to achieve objectives **7.3** Allocate work and evaluate teams, individuals and self against objectives **7.4** Provide feedback to teams and individuals on their performance
8.1 Establish and maintain the trust and support of one's staff **8.2** Establish and maintain the trust and support of one's immediate manager **8.3** Establish and maintain relationships with colleagues **8.4** Identify and minimize interpersonal conflict **8.5** Implement disciplinary and grievance procedures **8.6** Counsel staff
9.1 Obtain and evaluate information to aid decision making **9.2** Forecast trends and developments which affect objectives **9.3** Record and store information
10.1 Lead meetings and group discussions to solve problems and make decisions **10.2** Contribute to discussions to solve problems and make decisions **10.3** Advise and inform others

national database for vocational qualifications

1 – basic knowledge	2 – limited application	3 – varied application highly skilled

(depression) can bring about a lowering of self-esteem which makes you focus on what you cannot do, rather than on what you can do, and you will need the drive, stamina and self-confidence to get through the learning curve to become a high performing and task mature manager. You may also need resilience to get past the disappointments of not getting a proposal approved or not knowing all about 'how things are done around here', and a measure of assertiveness to get the help you need if it is not offered by the organization. Finally you will need determination to let go of the activities and attitudes of the past.

To use our swamp analogy again: if you were preparing to cross a swamp, surely you would take stock of the skills and equipment you already had which would provide you with a 'survival kit', get rid of any 'excess baggage' and learn as much as you could about the environment and how it might affect your journey. You would also need the self-confidence to believe you could do it and the determination to get to the other side.

Questionnaire: Transferable skills

1. List below three or four things that you do really well or skills that you are proud of.
   •
   •
   •
   •

2. Using the skills profile (in this chapter) or the management standards on pages 60–1 as a guide, how would you describe your key work-based strengths?
   •
   •
   •
   •

3. Which of the following words would you use to describe your key personal strengths?
   • Assertive.
   • Energetic.
   • Flexible.
   • Confident.
   • Resilient.
   • Trusting.

4. Thinking about your organization and the business it is in, how would you describe the following:
   • The emerging competencies.
   • The maturing competencies.
   • The transitional competencies.
   • The core competencies.

5. How does your own profile match this?

6. How might your profile need to change in the next year?

Chapter 6

Stepping stones

If you don't know where you are going any path will take you elsewhere. (SIOUX PROVERB)

Introduction

In preparing this book we asked several groups of professionals what, or who, helped (or could have helped) them in making the transition to management. The responses we got were very varied. The following are a few of the things they identified:

ILLUSTRATIONS

- 'I needed some induction – the time and space to absorb basic information and sort the practical issues.'
- 'I needed permission to prioritize.'
- 'Understanding organizational policies (the strategic view) was important.'
- 'Clear guidelines of what I was expected to achieve, by when, would have helped.'
- 'Someone to explain how to manage conflicting demands, i.e. negotiating skills.'
- 'I had a support system.'
- 'I wanted a team to belong to.'

Looking at the above list the following two kinds of help can be identified:

1. The kinds that are structured, planned and built into the way the organization works. They are like stepping stones or a planned route across the swamp, and are explored in this chapter.
2. Those which work on a more personal, specific or ad hoc level. These are like lifelines you can reach for if you reach a sticky patch or are in trouble, and are explored in Chapter 7.

Both lifelines and stepping stones should be available to enable people to maximize their competence and confidence as quickly as possible.

You may wish to use the information in the next two chapters to reflect on how well developed the sources of help are in your own organization, using the questions at the end of the chapters to plan how you might influence their development for the benefit of yourself and others.

Why might you need help?

You may have preconceived ideas about what a manager should be like. These might be based on (i) past experience of how you have been managed, (ii) people you know who are managers or (iii) from an academic or theoretical model.

There are always different perceptions about roles. Even if you have worked in the same organization, or the same part of it, for a number of years, what you expect of someone in a particular job and what other people expect of them will differ.

Figure 6.1 shows that there are potentially the following six definitions of every role:

1. *What is written in the job description*, which may be current or out of date. There may be new areas of responsibility or skills required since it was produced (such as using computers rather than manual systems to provide information).

2. *How the job holder interprets the role*. Everyone develops a role in the light of their own abilities and interests. They may be highly skilled

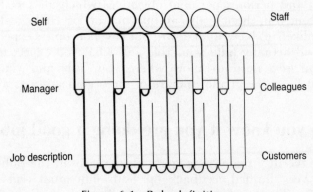

Figure 6.1   Role definitions

at, or prefer, some parts of the job and overachieve in those areas, whereas they may be not so good in, or actively dislike, other areas and do only the minimum in those areas.

3. *What the manager really expects* which may vary from both the job description and how the job holder interprets the role. The manager may have parts of her/his own job that are unpopular or that the subordinate has more experience of and may expect them to 'fill the gaps', or s/he may have difficulty letting go of a preferred activity which should really be part of the subordinate's job.

4. *Colleagues* will have a view of how the job should be done and how that job will interact with their own job. They may expect the job holder will need to be 'carried' or plan to exploit her/him, or they may be pleased to welcome the newcomer on equal terms as part of the team.

5. *Staff* may have a different interpretation again. They often expect from a new manager what they enjoyed (or suffered) under the predecessor. They may want more freedom or more guidance; to use her/his expertise or to develop their own; a great deal of involvement or little communication, and so forth.

6. *Internal and external customers* will also have expectations from the role holder dependent on the previous incumbent, their past experience of the new person or their experience of other suppliers.

The importance of perceptions

To survive the transition you need both the time and the opportunity to understand what these various expectations are and how you can meet or change them. This means that as well as a formal contract, job description and perhaps personal objectives which all specify what is expected from you, there is also an informal or 'psychological contract' which is unlikely to be written down, but covers people's expectations of how you will actually fulfil your role and what you expect of them in return. You also need to know where your role and your unit or department fit in the greater picture of the organization as a whole.

How do you know if you are doing a good job?

Until very recently many managers, particularly in the public sector, have had very limited feedback on both individual and corporate performance. This is changing dramatically with the introduction of performance standards and indicators and appraisal systems, which means many people are moving from a somewhat vague situation to one where they are subject to much more formal systems. They might also be expected to use strict (sometimes punitive) measures with staff who were previously colleagues and who may have been used to a much more relaxed management regime. Furthermore while some quantitative measures may be self-evident, they are rarely sufficient to give a complete assessment of the provision of services. Measures of quality are much harder to define and agree, and can frequently cause considerable friction between managers and staff.

Private sector organizations tend to have a clearer focus on performance, including well-established appraisal systems for managers to use, but individual managers can still find it very difficult to talk to another person about their performance. Clearly this can put a newly appointed manager under additional strain because (i) they may feel the need to justify their assessment of an ex-colleague's performance more forcefully than a more experienced manager would or (ii) they may be receiving specific feedback about their own performance for the first time.

The stepping stones

We have identified the following six key stepping stones for all new managers:

1. *Structure*. Where the manager's role fits in the department and organization.
2. *Selection*. The processes used to appoint or promote into management roles.
3. *Systems*. To define responsibilities, offer development and provide rewards.
4. *Standards*. To monitor and review performance for both individuals and teams.
5. *Skills*. Opportunities to build existing, and develop new, skills.
6. *Support*. For the individual at an organizational and a personal level.

(See Figure 6.2 for an illustration of the six stepping stones.)

1. Why is structure an issue?

Structure is an issue because many organizations grow or develop in unplanned ways. Departments or units are created for very good reasons (at the time it is done) but over a period of time any structure may become less logical. The relationship between departments can also

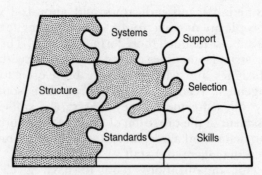

Figure 6.2   Stepping stones

change because their main areas of interest/responsibility develop which in turn has an impact on other departments. For example, the growth in the use of information technology may have changed the balance of responsibility between a central financial unit and other departments, or the increasing attention paid to quality management systems may have 'promoted' those people involved in quality testing from a production unit to quality assurance at boardroom level. Equally, some units become more significant because a particular individual in a key position or a specific project develops a high profile. All organizations should review the purpose, size and structure of a unit before appointing a new manager to it. This would include checking the relevance, appropriateness and size of the unit, the quantity of work and whether it has increased or decreased significantly, and whether the nature of work itself has changed. Does the unit still fit into the same part of the organization or should it be relocated?

At the same time, as a new manager you need to know where the unit or department fits into the overall scheme of things and what your role is as manager of that unit. Is the structure static or changing? Should it be changed to something which better reflects current business and priorities?

Many public sector organizations have traditionally been professionally driven. Staff appointed to junior or professional positions have been encouraged to develop through gaining qualifications and continuous professional development. In some organizations, apart from the most senior people who may have titles like Chief Executive or Director, many others have not been called managers. They could be Heads of Service, Principal Officers, Chief Engineer, Chief Fire Officer, Borough Solicitor, and so forth. Is your organization professionally based? What has been expected of the head of a department? Is it changing? Do new demands mean the organization needs a new structure? What is the role of its managers in the future? What will your role be?

> **ILLUSTRATION**
>
> From a head teacher of a large secondary school with responsibility for the budget for the school, 'I have to keep telling myself I'm not a teacher any more but the manager of a million pound business.'

2. Why is selection important?

We have already identified that some organizations expect to be able to recruit/promote people into managerial roles and get 100 per cent performance immediately (even 110 per cent from a young manager replacing a retiring one). Unfortunately the same organizations may still use recruitment and selection practices based on opinion rather than data. They may use no tests at all, or those based on personality rather than capability. The definition of the manager's role can still be based on traditional job descriptions with lists of tasks rather than focusing on results and consequently the key skills to achieve them. The move to using competency-based approaches to management discussed in the previous chapter may contribute to changing recruitment practices, but the use of competencies still may not be part of the mainstream management processes, including recruitment.

The following are the key stages in effective recruitment/selection:

1. Review the current job definition to see whether it is still relevant or needs changing.
2. Review the job description to see if it focuses on results or key areas of responsibility (what the holder is expected to achieve) rather than a list of tasks (things to do).
3. Produce a specification of the knowledge, skills, experience and qualifications needed for someone to be able to achieve those results and identify any particular criteria for taking up the job, for example, being willing to move to another site or country.
4. Advertise the job, highlighting what the person will be expected to do and what knowledge, skills, etc., they will need to be able to do it and inviting applications, or notify those people you want to apply or have nominated for the job.
5. Use a structured approach to assess each applicant against the specification. This may include tests to demonstrate competence as well as interviews.
6. Appoint the person who best fits the specification and meets the criteria.

For the organization, the benefit of this approach is that, while there are no guarantees, it may reduce the likelihood of a 'mismatch' between the new manager and the job requirements. Some people may still be promoted for more personal reasons, but at least that person should be capable of doing the job. Equally, the candidate may still be there because 'if I don't go for it, X will and I can't do worse than they would,' but at least s/he should know what is expected of her/him, and s/he can be confident that her/his skills and experience match the requirements of the new role. This 'systematic' type of approach should help to minimize the number of 'accidental' managers. How could it affect you?

3. Why are systems important?

Systems are important so that people know where they stand. If the selection processes are ad hoc or vary substantially between different parts of an organization, new managers and their colleagues and staff may have very little faith in their appointment. Using formal systems may seem laborious, but the investment is much more likely to give a good quality decision.

ILLUSTRATION

As one personnel manager told us -'If you are recruiting someone on £20,000 a year and expect they will stay for ten years, you are investing something like a quarter of a million pounds in that person. Can you afford to get it wrong?'

That investment is designed only to get the person appointed. It takes no account of the contribution s/he makes (or does not make) to the organization's goals once s/he has been appointed. You also need systems for ensuring the training and development of managers in their role. If a key feature of many organizations is rapid change, then managers need to be equipped to deal effectively with it. Clearly, training needs will vary between individuals, but having a system to regularly review needs and a framework for meeting them will increase the probability of managers keeping up to date and being more effective.

Managers also need to feel a sense of achievement and to be given recognition for their efforts (remember the motivating factors from Chapter 3). Effective reward systems are crucial in any organization. This means not only having good financial rewards or associated benefits which actually reflect the effort of individuals rather than just their status, but it should also include systems for setting clear performance criteria and giving helpful feedback on achievement against them. Where they exist, performance review systems do not always have a positive effect on those being reviewed and in the past many organizations have not had individual appraisals; however, we have never yet met anyone who said they did not want a clear sense of purpose and to know 'how they were doing' in their job.

ILLUSTRATION

As part of many training courses, we have asked hundreds of people to list two things that their manager did that (i) helped and (ii) hindered them from doing their own job well. The lists vary, but they always include the following:

1. Help:
   - 'Being given a clear idea what is expected of me, then being left to get on with it.'
   - 'Being there to ask for help, to discuss problems, but not interfering in my job.'
   - 'Knowing how I am doing.'
2. Hinder:
   - 'Being inconsistent about what s/he wants.'
   - 'Never being there.'
   - 'Not making decisions, but not letting me make them either.'

What systems are there in your organization and how do they impact on you?

4. Why are standards important?

Different organizations use different words, such as goals, objectives or targets, to describe how they set their expectations of employees. These may be defined loosely or using the SMART approach. Loosely written aims and objectives are of very little use and can be more frustrating than not having any at all because they are open to wide interpretation and frequently lead to misunderstanding. The alternative is to write them in such a way that they can be used to set direction, focus energy and effectively monitor and review individual and team performance. Objectives are SMART because they are the following:

- S – specific, clear and precise.
- M – measurable; achievement can be measured in terms of quality, quantity, time and/or cost.
- A – achievable and agreed by the person responsible for achieving them.
- R – relevant to the key areas of responsibility of the job.
- T – time related and traceable. Their achievement by a certain deadline can be verified.

In other words, the goals or objectives should be written so that they are practical and useful. If objectives are imposed but not agreed, there may be limited commitment to them, if they are not specific they could be misunderstood; and if they are not measurable and time related, how can the individual and the organization know if they have been achieved or not?

However, standards are also important. Performance is not finite and people are not machines. If performance varies from individual to individual it is important to know not only what is desirable (the ideal to aim for) but also what is essential or what must be achieved (the bottom line). Standards still need to be SMART because they are the minimum acceptable level of performance. Many organizations have goals but do not spell out the standards of performance they expect, even from managers. The management standards produced by MCI do not do this either. They specify *what* managers should be able to do and *in what circumstances*, but they do not say *how well*. Yet everyone needs to know how well they are doing their job.

Using SMART objectives and standards will also help new managers to focus how they spend their time. We know that one of the most difficult things to do as a manager is to get the balance right between different activities, as exemplified by the following questions: Are staff queries seen as an interruption to the job or the job itself (what you are there for)? Should you be spending time sorting out problems yourself or expect your subordinates to do it with only guidance from you (hands off)? How do you decide what to do when there are fifteen things all seemingly of the same importance? Therefore how should you spend your time?

The answer would depend on the key areas of responsibility in your job and their associated priorities. You either need to know what your manager thinks the priorities are or be allowed to set them yourself (as quoted in the list at the beginning of this chapter).

If an organization has induction for managers it would help clarify many of these concerns from the start.

5. The development of skills

Induction
Most organizations have some form of introductory process to help new members of staff to learn what is expected of them and how their job fits into the greater scheme of things. Induction would usually cover the following:

- The job and where you will work.
- The unit or department – what it does and how it works, who your colleagues are and what they do.
- The organization – what products or services it provides, how it is run and what the basic rules, systems and procedures are.

Many more organizations now recognize that it takes time to learn new skills and procedures and to acclimatize to your role, the people, the place and 'how we do things around here'. For new managers, however, there is rarely the opportunity to go through a similar process, or at least to cover all the elements in sufficient detail. This could be for a number of reasons, such as the following:

- The recruitment/promotion process has taken a long time, the job has been vacant and the unit had fallen behind in its work so that catching up is the priority.
- More senior managers are under so much pressure that they pass that pressure to perform straight to the new manager.
- Senior managers do not think that induction for people at management levels is necessary.
- They recognize it is necessary but feel you should be able to arrange it all for yourself.
- No one has thought about it.

Many managers are expected to perform immediately with very little or no time to clarify what their boss expects of them, get acquainted with their staff, catch up with what happened prior to their appointment and review how their unit fits with the rest of the organization. If you are pressurized to produce results too quickly it can be very easy to feel 'out of control' or 'on a roller coaster' and 'under stress' because you simply have not had the time or structured help to learn what to do. This is particularly true if the appointment to manager also means taking responsibility for a new building or new team of people.

Induction for managers should, at the minimum, include the following:

- A detailed discussion with your manager about her/his interpretation of the job, and what the priorities and boundaries of authority are in relation to her/his own role.
- A briefing of the key projects or work carried out recently.
- Time to meet your staff and get to know them.
- Time to read relevant documentation.
- Information about the key issues relating to the staff in your unit or department.

- An explanation of the main work and staff procedures (for example, booking holidays, recording absence and sickness, recruitment practices, dealing with discipline and grievance issues, etc.).
- Your key responsibilities for office premises/space, equipment, cleaning, security, and so forth.
- Relationships with other colleagues/departments including meetings to attend and/or people you need to consult.
- Key documentation or statistical returns you will be responsible for producing.
- How your budget is compiled, monitored and amended.

Clearly, it takes time to cover all the above issues, and being expected to perform in the job to 100 per cent immediately allows no time to adjust to the role, people and place. However, we know that many new managers who have been appointed to replace a retiring colleague are expected to perform better than their predecessor (110 per cent) or are expected to perform to the same high level of output (results) in their new role as they were achieving in their professional one. What approach does your organization have?

ILLUSTRATION

From a manager who was told on her appointment that 'a bright young thing like you should get things into shape in no time' found, however, 'there were so many queries to deal with during the day, I used to take piles of papers home each evening in an attempt to catch up with what had been happening, and who was doing what. It was like a roller coaster.'

To survive the transition from professional to manager you need time and space not only to adjust to your new environment but also to review and build on the skills brought with you from your professional background, and to identify and develop, through specific training, those you will need as a manager.

Specific training
Although many organizations now have training opportunities for managers, their value can vary enormously dependent on the content, style and timing of the training. There are a number of approaches which can be used based on the following two dimensions:

1. Whether the focus of the training is (i) long-term education/general development or (ii) specific knowledge and skills for immediate application.
2. Whether it is on the individual learning alone or within a group/ work team.

Standard (or academic) courses covering basic management principles give knowledge, insight and analytical skills, but may have lower short-term benefits than a tailor-made short course covering the specific knowledge and skills managers will be expected to use immediately. On the other hand, very short courses that focus on 'do this and you will be an excellent interviewer (or negotiator, etc.)' can take a superficial look at complex skills and give the participant confidence without understanding the implications of behaving in a particular way all the time. Different people benefit from different approaches.Training also needs to be given at an appropriate time. There is little point developing recruitment interviewing skills one year after a major recruitment exercise, or budgeting techniques if you will have no control over setting a budget for two more years.

Individuals learning alone or within a group or work team. This means how much solitude or interaction the learner has and how appropriate that is to (i) the topic being covered and (ii) the individual's preferred learning styles. Distance learning materials (and things like videos) provide a useful source of knowledge and the basis for developing problem-solving skills, but they may be of limited value in developing interpersonal skills where practice and feedback are so important. Obviously they are flexible so the learner can work at her/his own pace and tap into the materials at times which are convenient to her/him, rather than when a course has been scheduled.

Group work, on the other hand, is important for developing interpersonal skills and testing theories and assumptions, but it takes time and may not suit people who are timid, or are not comfortable communicating in a group. They can also be less than effective if there is too wide a range of ability and experience in the group. Effective training therefore would be based on the following:

• Designing opportunities to meet clearly identified, current needs.
• Events which are available at the 'right' time for a learner (that is, when the learning makes sense and can be put into practice).
• The content and pace being appropriate to the needs of individual learners.
• A course which has a mixture of skills development and the underpinning knowledge or theoretical background, so that participants learn what to do, how to do it and why they need to.

- Distance learning material which is easy to use with support available if it is not understood.
- The use of techniques/aids which are relevant for what is being learned.
- Effective briefing and de-briefing with your manager to help the transfer of learning back to work.

What opportunities are available to you?

ILLUSTRATIONS

From two graduate managers in a large manufacturing company:

- 'Yes we were offered a training course, but I'd already been doing the job for a year.'
- 'The management course I went on was very prestigious, but half the things they covered I already knew and the other half I will not be able to put into practice for years.'

Management development strategies and the learning company approach

The extent to which training for managers is embedded into the organization's culture will have a significant impact on its effectiveness. If the organization has a strategic view of management development, or genuinely lives by the principles of continuous development for the whole organization, then the needs of individual managers should be well catered for within that philosophy. However, at the point of writing there are very few organizations who would really embrace *all* the features of a 'learning organization'.

6. Organizational support

Good administrative and secretarial support can be invaluable for new managers, not only for the rapid transfer of essential information about systems and procedures, but to enable the new manager to settle into her/his new role quickly and effectively. They can introduce the manager to other staff and provide a 'buffer' to give the new person time and space to adjust to her/his role. Unfortunately there are examples of support staff who make things more difficult for their new manager than they need to be, as a sort of ritualistic test. What kind of support is available in your organization?

Pitfalls

Returning to our metaphor, without adequate direction or structures for crossing a swamp you will inevitably fall in. The lack of direction means that you may easily get distracted by things that are irritating but not important (like mosquitoes), or fall prey to those people who want to make things difficult so that you do not succeed (the alligators). That is when the alternative sources of help – the lifelines – then become most important. These sources of personal support are covered in the next chapter.

Questionnaire: What are the stepping stones in your organization?

1. How would you rate your organization for providing stepping stones for newly appointed managers? Rate the following stepping stones on a scale of 1 to 10.

	1 *low* ——— *high* 10
The structure of the organization is clearly defined.	1 2 3 4 5 6 7 8 9 10
The organization chart is up to date.	1 2 3 4 5 6 7 8 9 10
My role is clearly defined and understood.	1 2 3 4 5 6 7 8 9 10
We have effective recruitment systems.	1 2 3 4 5 6 7 8 9 10
Our reward system is appropriate and effective.	1 2 3 4 5 6 7 8 9 10
Our appraisal system is up to date and used effectively.	1 2 3 4 5 6 7 8 9 10
We have SMART objectives.	1 2 3 4 5 6 7 8 9 10
People are clear about the standards of performance they are expected to achieve.	1 2 3 4 5 6 7 8 9 10
We have good induction for all staff including managers.	1 2 3 4 5 6 7 8 9 10
Effective management training is available to all new managers.	1 2 3 4 5 6 7 8 9 10

New managers have sufficient administrative
and secretarial support.   1 2 3 4 5 6 7 8 9 10

2. What steps could be taken to improve the situation in future?

3. How might *you* influence the situation to enable the necessary changes to
    take place?

Chapter 7

Lifelines

*It can be no dishonour to learn from others, when
they speak good sense.* (SOPHOCLES 496–06 BC)

Introduction

Why might you feel the need for personal help?

Even in an organization with well-developed processes for new
managers, there may be a real need for additional mechanisms to
provide help for individuals at a more personal level. Do you remember
the concept of task maturity in Chapter 5? Despite being both competent
and confident in one role the feelings can quickly change as you move
into a new role. You may feel anxious or unsure which can lead to
overreacting – behaving very strongly or timidly, which can become
dysfunctional, getting yourself into a negative loop (see Figure 7.1). This
can be true for both men and women, but sometimes women managers
can feel that they have to try much harder and do much better than their
male colleagues, and not ask for help. This is particularly likely if they
are in a minority in the management hierarchy.

Various forms of help may enable you to move from a negative loop
to a positive loop. For example, training may contribute towards a
change in behaviour, and induction may help enormously in reducing
anxiety. At a more personal level a mentor can help you develop self-
esteem or a support group may help to generate more positive feelings.

We are not suggesting that lifelines are any less valuable than
stepping stones, but if an organization does not have a planned
approach to developing managers, then more personal support systems
may be crucial in helping an individual to survive the transition to
management. Do you know what support is available in your
organization? If there is very little, how might you use the ideas in this
chapter to focus your energies in developing them for yourself?

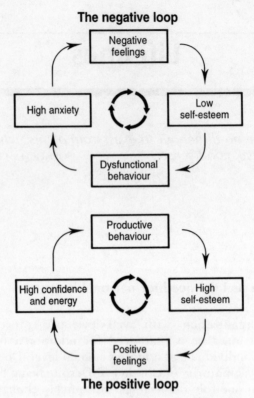

Figure 7.1   Confidence cycles

The lifelines

We have identified the following eight key lifelines for new managers:

1. Networking or support groups.
2. Action learning sets.
3. Coaching and getting positive feedback.
4. Mentoring.
5. Project work.
6. Shadowing.
7. Counselling.
8. Stress management.

(See Figure 7.2 for an illustration of these eight key lifelines.)

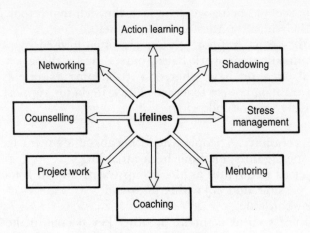

Figure 7.2   Lifelines

1. Networking or support groups

In our workshops, many ex-professionals said that one of the hardest things to 'let go of ' was the sense of belonging to a group, a team or the 'club'. You can no longer be 'one of the gang', and it can be very difficult to share your problems or have personal discussions with your staff. It can feel like you are on your own. If becoming a manager also means a move to a new location, an 'area' office or a new school, then the sense of isolation can be even more powerful.

> **ILLUSTRATION**
>
> From a head teacher, 'The worst thing about this job is it is so incredibly lonely. As a Head of Department you have colleagues, as the deputy you have the Head, as the Head . . . you are on your own.'

For many people, the idea of networking or support groups may be particularly associated with women's groups, but both men and women managers told us how much they would have, or did, value a support group with whom they could talk. The feeling that you cannot talk to the people immediately around you at work was very strong. You cannot talk to your staff because 'they expect you to have all the answers', nor colleagues because 'they may be competing with you for resources or future jobs' and not your own manager because 'it would be seen as weakness and damage your opportunities for promotion'. Yet these managers had a real need to talk through their perceptions of situations, share ideas and possible courses of action, and a forum in which to do it.

They did not see it as being weak; in fact, they felt that it took courage to face up to their uncertainties and ask for help.

Where they exist, support groups are often formed by people from similar organizations or work backgrounds, or by those who live in a geographical area or have shared a particular experience such as attending a training course together. The criteria for support groups to work effectively are the following:

- They are voluntary – people attend because they want to.
- The members gain something from attending.
- They meet as frequently as the group wants and in a location that makes it possible and enjoyable to attend.
- They are affordable.
- They are not seen as a threat by other key people in the members' lives.
- They deal with real issues honestly – no one 'plays games'.

ILLUSTRATIONS

From a group which has been meeting twice a year for seven years, 'We are far enough apart not to know the key players or have a vested interest in the issues or outcomes for one member, but close enough to care and want to help each other solve problems and deal with difficulties at work.'

From a health service manager, 'We soon agreed that the area meetings had two purposes: (i) to conduct the formal business and (ii) 'time out' to talk through problems and share ideas.'

From the manager of his own small company 'It would be great to have a group to share problems and discuss options with.'

---

2. Action learning sets

Action learning sets are similar to networks but are particularly focused on learning. Their purpose has been described as 'to encourage managers to find their bearings quickly, in situations of confusion and obscurity where there is neither initial agreement about, nor under-standing of, what to do for the best' (Casey and Pearce 1977). They were originally developed as an alternative to traditional management training courses and are based on the philosophy that people learn better by working on live issues in the real environment, which means they need to undertake specific actions to solve problems and create changes. This is because they learn not only about the specific situation but also about themselves. In other words, action learning is 'learning by doing', where individual managers over a period of several months, take on a project to solve a real work problem. The problems are normally organizational, not technical, current and something that had no obvious solution. You belong to a small group or 'set' which meets regularly, usually once a week, together with a facilitator (set advisor) to help each other diagnose the real problems, recommend and follow through action to solve them.

More recently action learning sets have been developed to be the part of a management training process which continues after a course has finished. They can be arranged within one organization or from a mixed group. Each member brings to the 'set' a live issue, problem or project that s/he wishes to work on. Through regular meetings the members help each other work on the issue and learn from their experience with it. The role of the set advisor is to facilitate learning, helping the members of the group to focus on learning from what they are doing, both in terms of the particular issues and the way the group is working together.

ILLUSTRATION

From a senior manager, 'Using the action learning set on a management training course to help think things through was a real help.'

To be effective action learning sets should be as follows:

- Small (approximately five members).
- Diverse with different organizations, cultures, roles and skills represented.
- Egalitarian in managerial level, intellectual and emotional strength, and capacity and challenge in the projects (members need to respect each other, in order to give and receive help).
- Able to provide enough drive for the projects to be progressed.
- Led by skilled facilitators who are good at understanding managerial issues, timing useful contributions (such as asking questions), being truthful but helpful, and most important, keeping quiet. (Technical expertise and traditional training skills such as preparation, structuring and presentation are not appropriate for this role.) Advisors also need to be tolerant of ambiguity and have both empathy and patience to work on the individual issues at the pace of the participants.
- Voluntary because not everyone finds this approach helpful; some managers find it too much like floundering in the dark.

- Biased to organizational (not technical) problems so that there is some opportunity for cross learning.

3. Coaching

The benefits of coaching are well known in sport, where it is extensively practised, but while being a very powerful tool, it is frequently underrated in the work context. There are many reasons for this, such as the following:

- The more senior manager not having the time.
- S/he is reluctant to discuss the development needs of a subordinate in order to avoid what could be seen as criticism.
- In the past, many organizations (especially in industry) have been organized in a 'command and control' way and there is often a sense that 'managers must manage', i.e. subordinates must be told what to do, rather than encouraged to work things out for themselves.

While the first two reasons may still exist there is an increasing realization that there are alternative, and more effective, ways of managing people than simply 'telling them'. In this sense, effective coaching means the following:

- The coach is interested in the 'protégé', knowing her/his interests, aims and capabilities, and actively looks for her/his potential.
- The coach recognizes the existing skills and abilities of the learner and builds on them to enhance performance ('showing confidence in the protégé but expecting it to be justified').
- Both parties have the same objectives in mind.
- There is a close relationship of mutual trust and respect.
- (Normally) the coach has more experience than the learner, but does not use it in a 'dictatorial' or 'telling' style. Instead s/he should be able to explain or demonstrate a task, skill or process clearly and simply, then encourage the learner to ask questions and take responsibility for putting the learning into practice. The coach's role is one of giving encouragement and helpful feedback.

The last point is crucial as many people can give examples of lack of clear guidance (coaching) from their manager: for example, have you had any of these experiences when asked to write a report?

1. You have been left to do it without any help, then your first draft is 'attacked with the red pen'.

2. You were left to produce the report and pass it to senior management with no involvement.
3. Your manager stood over your shoulder telling you what to do at every stage.
4. S/he re-wrote it for you!!

In the above case an effective coach would do the following:

*   Gain your agreement to writing the report.
*   Discuss key features and stages and listen to any queries you have.
*   Leave you to produce the first draft.
*   Be available to discuss it, ask questions, listen to ideas and/or suggest changes.
*   Discuss it a second time.
*   Gradually leave you to do more and only check the end product.
*   When you are fully confident and competent leave you to do it.

The following are the four key stages to effective coaching:

1. *Presenting* the key information clearly, precisely and in language which the learner can understand, or demonstrating a task explaining at each stage what you are doing and why.

2. *Asking questions and listening* to stimulate thinking and check the level of interest and understanding of the learner (prompting their involvement if it is not readily offered), and encouraging them to raise concerns/queries to discuss.

3. *Observing and giving feedback* on how the learner performs a task for themselves and to what standard (note that they may need time to get it 'right first time' or to perform 'at speed'), then reviewing their performance and giving additional knowledge/support and feedback to enhance it.

4. *Agreeing further action* to sustain development.

Giving feedback

We would like to highlight this stage in particular because so many people feel that it is missing from their workplace.

If you are involved in a sport or playing a musical instrument, getting it wrong it can be very obvious because the ball does not go where it should, or the notes played do not produce the expected tune. In many areas of management the effects of your actions, or lack of skill, are much harder to define unless someone actively gives you feedback.

At the same time, in most organizations, day-to-day 'helpful' feedback from more senior managers is rare. You may have to ask for it.

Feedback is a way of helping a person to consider refining her/his behaviour by communicating information about how that behaviour affects others. Its purpose is to help someone keep 'on target' and be better able to achieve their goals. Most feedback is *not* helpful so has quite the opposite effect, creating defensiveness and tension. For feedback to be effective it should be the following:

• Descriptive not evaluative. The person giving it should act as a mirror not a judge by helping someone to see her/himself objectively and unemotionally, instead of creating defensiveness by sitting in judgement on her/him.
• Specific not general. To be told you are 'dominating' will probably be far less useful than being told 'when this point was being discussed you did not listen to what other people said, and I felt forced to accept your argument or be attacked by you.'
• Focused on visible behaviour not supposed mental states or personality. This means discussing what can be *seen*, what someone *does* and the *effects* of their actions, not what you believe they feel, think or want: it is not helpful to say things like 'you should be an inch taller.'
• Feedback should be directed towards behaviour that the person can do something about.
• Positive not negative. Emphasizing what someone should do differently instead of simply saying what has been done poorly; criticism without specific suggestions for improvements simply creates frustration and defensiveness without helping the person to improve. A problem-solving approach which adds action to descriptive information is more successful.
• Balancing the needs of the receiver as well as the giver. Feedback will be destructive if it is given because of the giver's needs to say something, and s/he does not consider the needs of the person receiving the comments.
• Well timed. This means at the earliest opportunity after the given behaviour (depending on the person's readiness to hear it).
• Solicited rather than imposed. This means it is much better if it is asked for or there is a degree of self-review.
• Communicated clearly and in appropriate amounts, so that what was heard was what was intended. It works best in a positive relationship (otherwise the feedback may be rejected.)

In response the receiver needs to:

• Be open minded. There is no point in 'playing games', if good feedback is hard to get, it should be valued.

- Ask questions to be sure s/he understands what is being said. The person giving feedback may be uncomfortable in that role or use language which is not quite clear in an attempt not to offend.
- Avoid arguing, interrupting or justifying her/his actions. The receiver should try not to be defensive, but listen carefully to what is being said, taking the information in the spirit of being helped.
- Accept feedback as a gift, even a right. It is an opportunity (not a threat) to improve her/his performance and understanding of individual behaviours and their consequences.
- Make up her/his own mind in deciding whether to act upon the feedback or not.

ILLUSTRATION

From a young graduate manager, 'The only feedback you get here is a real rollicking if things go wrong.'

---

4. Mentoring

Formal mentoring for managers is not widely found in organizations either. However, where it does exist it is usually highly valued, and many very successful people have said that they owed their success, at least in part, to a particular individual, whose advice and help had been invaluable in developing their career.

Mentoring comes from the idea of apprenticeship, where a senior, or more experienced manager, acts as role model, guide, tutor, coach and confidant for a younger person, or protégé, giving them support and confidence in developing her/his career. There are parallel approaches in many professions such as the careers service, and social work, where newly qualified staff are appointed but with a 'probationary' period during which time they must have a 'supervisor' to guide and tutor them. This may be a more prescribed process where it is expected that the relationship will be with the line manager and will have a clear element of 'supervision' but there are similarities in terms of the support and development expected from the role.

What are the benefits of mentoring?
There are many potential benefits. Each partner can profit from the relationship. The mentor may gain the following:

- New knowledge or skills to prevent burnout.
- A better relationship with the protégé's department or function.
- A way of absorbing extra work.

The protégé may gain the following:

- Encouragement and advice.
- Easier access to senior management.
- An opportunity for visibility through special assignments.
- Exposure to decision makers and their strategic thinking.
- Insights into organizational politics.
- Support and help with difficult assignments.

However, the mentoring process requires sensitive senior management involvement as it is not without its difficulties as Clark (1992) identified. Problems are likely to occur if:

- The mentor is seen to have more influence than the reporting manager.
- There is a lack of understanding or jealousy by the protégé's peers (or partner).
- The protégé becomes over-dependent on the mentor.
- The mentor uses the protégé to build her/his political empire.
- Unrealistic expectations are created.
- The mentor leaves the company unexpectedly.
- The mentor is within the organization and they are involved in the issue being explored.
- Interpersonal differences exist or develop between the mentor and protégé.

Although these difficulties can be overcome, they might help to explain why mentoring is not widely used. To overcome these difficulties and be effective mentoring should:

- Be a special relationship outside the boss–subordinate relationship. The mentor may get involved in helping the protégé to understanding how the organization works; and how to assess alternative courses of action, influence the decision makers and therefore get things done. It can be argued, therefore, that it should not be the line manager or even a manager in the same department (where there may be a conflict of interests).
- Focus on what makes an effective manager.
- Include discussions about the protégé's aspirations and development.
- Have set objectives and a process for monitoring progress.
- Be based on the active agreement of two people who can really relate to each other ('they have to choose each other' by matching needs and interests).

- Have a mentor who is actively committed to the process and is responsive to the protégé's needs and agenda.
- Have top management commitment together with a support system.
- Be established after both parties have been trained in their respective roles.
- Have time for the relationship to develop and issues to be explored.
- Be based on respect and confidentiality.
- Be able to end positively.

ILLUSTRATION

From a deputy head teacher, 'Without the (mentoring) programme I would not have had anyone to go to.'

From a manager, 'The most helpful thing was having a senior manager (not my line manager) to talk to.'

From a woman manager, 'My manager has identified that I need to take a more strategic view of things, so I need to talk to someone with more experience (preferably from outside the organization) who can help me do that.'

Mentoring may be particularly helpful to young women managers because (i) it gives direct access to key executives, (ii) it can increase their visibility in male dominated hierarchies and (iii) it should create a 'safe' relationship to share ideas and discuss problems which might not exist with a line manager.

5. Project work

One of the problems of moving into any new role is -'How do you know what it will really be like until you actually do it?' One approach might be to undertake a specific piece of real work to find out some of the features of that role (although obviously not all of them). One Health Service manager we spoke to had an active policy of encouraging potential managers to take on limited-term projects based on work that needed doing any way, but that would give the individual the opportunity to learn about management in the Health Service before committing her/himself to doing it.

Taking on projects can enable you to do the following:

- Get a broader view of how the organization works.
- Develop some managerial skills.

- Gain confidence without pressure.
- Have the opportunity to say 'this is not for me' without you or the organization having invested too much to turn back.

Projects are frequently an element of other forms of development, for example, a requirement as part of a qualification or management course. This can cause difficulties if there are a number of students all needing to find something to investigate. What happens then is that projects are often 'created' because there is a need to do 'something' which can lead to a belief that they are of very little use, and therefore there is virtually no commitment to their findings. As a result they can be greatly underrated as a part of a development strategy.

Projects should be the following to be effective:

- Based on real issues, problems or changes.
- Current not historical (unless they are a review of past action).
- Something that the individual and the organization have a real interest in addressing.
- Agreed with and supported by senior management.
- Given time. They should be conducted in a realistic time scale and balanced with the other job demands of the person doing it.
- Realistic but challenging. They should be matched to the ability of the individual.
- Based on the understanding that the suggested ideas and recommendations will be implemented or at least given serious consideration by the organization.

6. Shadowing

Shadowing is a process where someone from one organization or department spends a specified period of time with an experienced manager from another organization or department. Like a shadow they follow the individual through their normal work pattern, experiencing the same things and then taking time to share ideas and perceptions of those experiences. It can be a very successful way for new or potential managers to gain insight into the management role without the pressure or responsibility of actually doing it. To be effective shadowing needs the following:

- The 'shadowed' manager to be both willing and able to give the time to discussing the working day with the 'shadow'.
- A positive and helpful relationship between the parties.
- To be for a defined period of time.

- Clear guidelines on the expectations each party has of the other.
- A clear process for reviewing the time spent together and a measure or measures for success (why it was time well spent).
- The shadow to be willing to give feedback to the manager s/he is with or share her/his learning with other shadows.
- Everyone involved to understand their roles.
- A clear agreement about maintaining confidentiality.

7. Counselling

In some organizations there is a structured process for helping individuals plan and manage their careers which is called career counselling. However, the kind of counselling we are referring to is a lifeline or help available in response to a specific need.

Counselling is the process where one person helps another to deal with a particular problem that is concerning them, encouraging them to think through the issues, generate possible solutions and then facilitating any action. It may include personal as well as work issues and is different to many of the previous approaches because it *must* be led by the person with the problem ('the counsellee'). If they do not recognize the need for, or want, help, then it is totally inappropriate.

Everyone has emotions and when someone feels that they have a real problem then their emotions will usually be heightened. Different emotions may be felt and displayed, for example, frustration, anger, fear, panic or determination. The counsellor must be able to deal with them both professionally and supportively.

The key skills for counselling are the following:

- Listening.
- Reflecting.
- Summarizing.
- Giving helpful feedback.
- Problem solving.

The counsellor should never tell the counsellee what to do, and only offer advice if it is asked for or if, towards the end of the discussion, the other person still cannot see a way forward at all. Counselling is normally a fairly short-term relationship otherwise it may encourage dependence (where the counsellee begins to rely on the counsellor rather than gain confidence to deal with things her/himself). If counselling is available when needed and offered in a skilled and sensitive way, it can be a very powerful aid to people making decisions that they will stick to, and to real personal growth and development particularly for newly appointed managers.

Effective counselling depends on the following:

The counsellor:

- Having the analytical skills to help diagnose the issues.
- Having communication skills to help explore the issue, deal with emotions and generate action.
- Being able to show empathy and genuine willingness to help.
- Not jumping to conclusions but enabling the counsellee to work through the problem for her/himself.

The counsellee:

- Recognizing there is a problem and being willing to address it.

Both parties:

- Having the time and opportunity to discuss the issue in a private and unhurried way.
- Having a positive relationship, with rapport, openness and honesty.
- Knowing when and how to 'disengage' from the process.

8. Stress management

For some people making the transition from professional to manager may be more than uncomfortable, it may lead to real stress. Stress can be defined in different ways including 'the point at which the pressures in your daily life become uncomfortable and unproductive, disabling you rather than stimulating energy' and 'the way in which your body reacts to these pressures'.

We all need an amount of pressure to stimulate us into doing anything and the body is designed to cope with short-term increases in those pressures, but if the pressure is too great or sustained over a long period of time it can lead to stress. Research has shown that change itself (whether positive or negative) can create stress, but because an individual's tolerance or enjoyment of change varies, so does her/his 'stress threshold'. The same research shows that some kinds of change are consistently more stressful than others, and a change in career or job ranks high on most lists of stressors after major changes in personal relationships, such as bereavement, marriage, divorce, severe illness or personal injury.

Stress can be experienced in different ways, such as difficulty in relaxing or sleeping, an increase in smoking or drinking, digestive or skin problems, irritability, difficulty in retaining information or making decisions, or being more argumentative or emotional in dealing with others. Recognizing that you are under stress is the first and most important step. Many people do not acknowledge that there is a problem until the physical symptoms become very severe and even then may be reluctant to accept that they need help because they fear it may be seen as weak.

Managing stress means the following:

- Recognizing the symptoms which show that you are under stress.
- Identifying those features or events in your life which generate an unacceptable level of pressure.
- Wanting to do something about them.
- Planning a range of actions to alleviate the effects of stress or eliminate the sources of it. These might include the following:
  (a) learning to relax;
  (b) adapting your eating, drinking and exercise regime to develop a healthier lifestyle;
  (c) making changes in your personal life to improve relationships;
  (d) looking for changes in routines, expectations and levels of support at work;
  (e) finding ways to manage your time more productively.

In many organizations there is a real reluctance to acknowledge either that managers experience stress or that it should be addressed. It may depend on people outside work to offer support and practical help to deal with it, for example, from a supportive partner, family or friend, or using the services of one of the help professionals.

Special issues for women

As mentioned at the beginning of the chapter there may be some issues of moving into management that are particularly problematic for women. A survey of the membership of the British Institute of Management (BIM) (Nicholson and West 1988) confirmed what most people would suspect, that although women are found in all areas of management, they are scarce at top levels and on Boards of Directors. Moreover, women are scarce in such areas as production, chemistry, engineering, financial and technical services compared with the sectors concerned with the caring professions (Clark 1992).

The survey found that a career in management still means, that while marriage and a family are supportive structures for men, they are obstacles for women. Many more women than before are foregoing marriage and family life in favour of their careers. A key finding was that women managers also tended to follow different career paths compared to men. They were educated to higher levels, occupying specialist positions at every point in the hierarchy. They tended to move faster

between jobs and made more radical changes (spiralling up and out),
and they maintained this pattern more or less continuously throughout
their careers. They were said to have high growth needs, were
intrinsically motivated and self-directed. This would be supported by
White, Cox and Cooper's research (1992) with forty-eight highly
successful women which identified the following values (or 'career
orientations' or 'anchors'):

- None of the women placed a high priority on getting to the top of their
  organizational hierarchy (getting ahead) although it could be argued
  that they had already done so, and their responses might have been
  different earlier in their careers.
- Nearly a third did say that they wanted recognition for their
  achievements, although this was seen as a personal value rather than
  the need to be re-assured that the organization valued them. The need
  for security (getting secure) was not strong, rather they saw
  themselves as risk takers. Twenty per cent of the women said that they
  had taken career moves which had appeared risky but had paid
  dividends.
- Forty-eight per cent had a strong orientation for challenge, interest
  and variety in their work while at the same time striving for the top
  (getting high).
- Fifteen per cent valued freedom and independence in their work
  (getting free) being prepared to challenge a job description, carve
  their own niche and/or opt for self-employment.
- The evidence did not show that these highly successful women placed
  a priority on balancing work and home (getting balanced) as work
  played a central role in their lives.

The BIM survey found that, in contrast, their male counterparts were
found to be more materialistic, goal and status oriented. In this survey
the women saw themselves as discriminated against by organizational
policies and made these radical moves upwards as a means of being less
subject to prejudice.

   While recognizing that many organizations and individuals are
working to address the issues of equality of opportunity, many women
clearly feel that they must try harder and perform better than their male
counterparts to reach the same levels in the hierarchy. There is also
evidence that organizations can expect strong conformity and show
limited tolerance of the process of managing the boundary between
home and work, which can be harder on women than men.

ILLUSTRATIONS

From three women managers:
- 'With two children it is difficult to find time to do everything – and there are very few opportunities for job share in management.'
- 'The thing I really hated was the expectation I would join the others at the pub every Friday.'
- 'Christmas is a nightmare – there are just too many things going on, trying to attend all the children's activities and those at work is horrendous.'

From a physiotherapist, 'I suddenly realized I had nothing to wear, all my working clothes were track suits, as a manager I was expected to come to work in a suit, it cost a fortune to make the change.'

What are the issues for women?

It seems that either individual women have very different orientations or that they have to make difficult choices about their roles. Three key issues are the following:

1. *Asking or not asking for help.* In an earlier chapter we identified that one of the stereotypes of managers is that they know the answers to all questions now. Other research has shown that many women are more comfortable with a consultative style of working rather than an authoritative one. However, if the working environment is one where the image of managers is to be strong, knowledgeable, sure of yourself and decisive, it can be very difficult for any new manager to ask for help. This is true for many men, but women may feel an additional pressure to be seen to conform to a style which is not their preferred one and which would include not being able to ask for help.

2. *Overcompensating.* There are other examples of women who conform to the image of strength to excess. Their behaviour is very forceful and aggressive because they believe (or have been told) that is what is expected of them in a managerial role. This can often create resentment from colleagues and staff; if it is not the natural style for the individual, then it can also lead to real stress in acting a part at work which is alien to your normal pattern of behaviour. If this is carried across to a family situation it can create stress in those relationships too.

3. *Managing the boundary of home and work.* For those women with dual roles this can be particularly difficult for women for the following reasons:

(a) the need to be single minded because management is considered to be more competitive than many other professions. In. some organizations, competition between colleagues is actively encouraged to stimulate better performance. However, if the effect of this competition is to create an atmosphere where people are reluctant or fearful to share ideas, problems and concerns, it may encourage an attitude that you only get on by 'treading all over' others, and being totally single minded and committed to your own success. This will leave little room for relationships which do not contribute to that success;

(b) the existence of 'group rules'. In some organizations there are unwritten social rules, such as going to the pub every Friday night after work, or all belonging to a particular club or sports centre. If the majority of managers are men it may be more difficult (or quite inappropriate) for women managers to 'join the club'. They may not want to go to the pub, or prefer other sports or activities, but not conforming can have the effect of excluding you from your peer group;

(c) inflexible or very demanding working patterns. As quoted in our last illustration 'there are very few opportunities for job share as a manager.' Not only are managers expected to work full time they are frequently expected to put in additional hours or travel on a regular basis or at short notice. This can be more difficult if you have primary responsibility for child care or other dependent relatives;

(d) Career breaks are becoming more accepted, but for a woman returning to work after a break of four, five or more years, they may well be four years behind colleagues on the career ladder. Alternatively, they may find that they are expected to return to work at a lower level than they left. One of the advantages of the developing interest in competencies is that you may be able to demonstrate competence from non-work activity (such as setting up and managing a nursery or play group) and have your managerial abilities recognized more readily by an employer.

Questionnaire: What lifelines would be most helpful for you?

Looking at you own situation, complete the following:

1. Identify the key features of your professional role and then of your new (or potential) managerial situation. For example: How isolated might you feel (and therefore value a support group)? How many new situations might you need to manage (where an action learning set or project work could help)? Are there more senior managers who have previously been in a similar situation who may be willing to coach or mentor you?
2. Thinking also about your own approach to change and personal circumstances, identify what you think are the most important developmental and personal needs you have now or might have in the next six to twelve months.
3. Using any relevant previous experience and the information in this chapter, highlight the most appropriate mechanisms to support you during this period.

Professional role	Management role	Development/ personal needs	Best method of support

Chapter 8

The new island
Managing in the year 2000

All is flux . . . Therefore you cannot step twice in the same river. (HERACLITUS 535–475 BC)

Introduction

There are many models of management which have been developed during the twentieth century, including scientific, humanist and systems models, those focusing on change and those emphasizing excellence in quality and service. Managing change has been seen as a key feature of successful management for some time. However, the traditional approach to change in which management describes the manager like the captain of a ship sailing through calm seas, seeing a storm, successfully navigating through it and then returning to calm waters again, no longer holds true. A senior manager recently described his role as being 'more like white water rafting, than sailing a calm sea'. In future the result of change is highly unlikely to be a new safe and secure island, and managers will need new skills to manage rapid and complex change in an increasingly turbulent environment.

Gareth Morgan (1988) says, 'More than ever the world is in flux. And organizations and their managers must recognise the necessity of developing the mindsets, skills and abilities that will allow them to cope with this flux.' These qualities include anticipating environmental trends, developing 'proactive mindsets', developing and sharing a vision, and empowering others to perform without strong control structures. Increasingly, managers will need to promote creativity and learning, effectively use the data which have become available with the information technology (IT) revolution, and learn to live with complexity and ambiguity. For many managers (particularly in more traditional organizations), this may require them not only to develop new skills and competencies, but also to challenge the underlying assumptions with which they have managed people. It also means an increased preparedness to take 'calculated' risks. This new island,

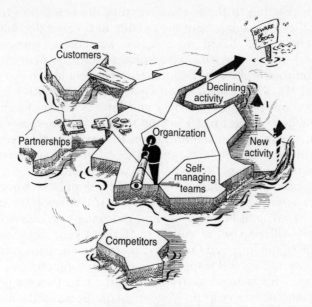

Figure 8.1   The new island

therefore, will have limited 'firm ground' and its foundations will be under constant threat of erosion (see Figure 8.1).

Six areas of management focus

To deal with this threat we believe that effective managers will need to focus on the following six areas:

1.   The environment.
2.   The shape of the organization.
3.   The management role.
4.   Culture or the psychological contract.
5.   Individual and team development.
6.   Calculated risks and real-time learning.

1. The environment

A manager will need to constantly collect, analyze and use information to assess the environment within which s/he is working. S/he will need to respond rapidly to change, perhaps seeking opportunities for work rather than reacting to them, thus creating the new firm ground. This has been called managing from the outside in (i.e. not deciding what we can or want to do based on internal structures, competence and perspectives; but seeing what customers require; anticipating change, then developing the skills and approaches that enable you to respond to their needs). In *The Empty Raincoat* Charles Handy (1994) refers to the need to plan new products, services and futures before the current ones go into decline. In the private sector there are numerous examples of how organizations have taken initiatives to maximize their relationships with customers and suppliers, and to develop their understanding of their markets in attempts to anticipate future needs.

In the public sector, the introduction of compulsory competition for some professional, as well as direct, services will develop the same focus. This can mean responding to a client or customer who may seem to have a completely different set of values to those of your organization. The introduction of the 'internal market' can create a situation, especially for managers, where they feel trapped between two conflicting views of what is important. This is particularly likely if the client seems preoccupied with the *quantity* of service at the expense of quality, and the professionals want to focus on *quality*.

2. The shape of the organization

Traditionally, as organizations have grown they have become more hierarchical and this is usually represented by an organization chart like a family tree. We now accept that while these structures have been appropriate for 'steady state' production or more predictable service provision, they are now rarely able to react quickly enough to rapid changes in customer needs or the environment. Flatter and more flexible organizations are needed, made up of a network of teams. Survival may mean not being a clearly defined island, but a network of interdependent communities linked to other groups in a variety of ways. Organizations may become looser federations of teams. These teams may also need to build new relationships, partnerships or bridges to other organizations in which case the role of management will become more focused on enabling the individuals and teams to perform by managing the interface between the organization and its environment, rather than having a predominantly internal perspective.

3. The management role

As we know from Henry Mintzberg's research (see Chapter 1) managers already sit between the organization and a network of contacts. As the emphasis shifts to managing from the outside in, managers will need to keep in closer touch with what is going on in their environments, manage many initiatives and also balance the conflicting interests of multiple stakeholders. This means learning to live with uncertainty and developing approaches to managing complexity and ambiguity.

At the same time, with an increased demand to focus outside the organization, managers may not be able to spend as much time in their role as resource allocators and monitors. This means that they cannot afford to get too involved in the specific tasks of their staff so they will need to develop the skills to keep a strategic overview of activities without being involved in the detail. Many people describe this as losing touch with the day-to-day work of their staff. As one manager told us, 'I can't do what they do any more, I'm not even sure how the system works.'

4. Culture or the psychological contract

To be successful in a rapidly changing environment we may also need to question the basic assumptions about 'the understanding that people have, whether written or unwritten, regarding the commitments made between themselves and their organization' (Rousseau 1994). As a result of rapid and fundamental change in organizations, the traditional assumptions about security of employment, fairness and relationships are no longer safe. As shown in the following feedback, there is a clear shift from collectivism to individuality in employment. Every manager becomes more personally accountable for her/his own performance and the results of her/his team within a context of constant pressure to improve.

The new psychological contract

From a survey of 104 managers asked to describe the relationship between employer and employee (Hiltrop 1995):

Past	Present
Long term	Immediate results
Security	Flexibility
Predictability	Uncertainty
Equality	Individuality
Certainty	High risk
Tradition	Constant change
Fairness	Personal gain
Stability	Employability
Interdependence	Self-reliance

Mutual trust	Opportunism
Company loyalty	Professional loyalty
Doing well	Doing better
Shared responsibility	Personal accountability
Title and rank	Making a difference
Pay for status	Pay for results
Tolerance	Impatience
Mutual respect	Fear

If these are the features of a new psychological contract, then managers will need to adapt their expectations of the organization accordingly and everyone will need to become more self-reliant. According to William Bridges (1994), author of the best-selling *Job Shift*, security now resides in the person rather than the position, and to a cluster of qualities that have nothing to do with the organization's policies or practices. He argues that from now on you will have a harder and harder time finding security in a job. In the future your security will depend on your developing the following three characteristics as a worker and as a person:

1. *Employability*. Your security will come first and foremost from being an attractive prospect to employers, and that attractiveness involves having the abilities and attitudes that an employer needs at the moment.

2. *Vendor-mindedness*. Being a traditional, loyal employee is no longer an asset. It has, in fact, turned into a liability. So you will need to stop thinking like an employee and start thinking like an external vendor who has been hired to accomplish a specific task.

3. *Resiliency*. Organizations today operate in such a turbulent environment that no arrangement works for them for very long. What you will need (both for the organization's sake and for your own) is the ability to bend and not break, to let go of the outdated and learn the new, to bounce back quickly from disappointment, to live with high levels of uncertainty and to find your security from within rather than from outside.

These abilities and attitudes will provide you with the only kind of security that exists today because they will fit you for what is going to be the work world of the foreseeable future: the project and an organization built around a changing mix of projects.

5. Individual and team development

Given this backcloth, everyone will also need to develop the new self-reliance and the skills to undertake new tasks. The competency-based approach has been slower to develop in management than in other areas of work and where it does exist it tends to be more focused on gaining qualifications than building performance. However, if in future, managers (as well as other grades of staff) need to (i) prove their capability and (ii) move quickly into new roles or organizations, the value of being able to demonstrate their competence through a collected portfolio of evidence, which meets nationally recognized standards, will enhance both their employability and confidence. With rapidly changing ground rules, learning from experience will also become a crucial skill for managers and staff alike.

This may represent another 'culture' change – to one of continuous development. If managers will have to be more concerned with strategy and boundaries, individuals and teams will need to develop both the skills and appropriate attitudes to become self-managing. Empowerment is currently a popular concept but it is considerably easier to label than to live. For it to be effective, empowerment requires genuine trust and support from management, together with considerable willingness and capability from staff. The manager still co-ordinates the results from different groups, but the groups have to take the initiative for defining and solving problems and responsibility for their own performance. This leads to the need for high performing and largely self-managing teams.

6. Calculated risks and real-time learning

Another key feature of the managing in the future will be the pressure of time. With the quantity and variety of demands made on managers, they will have to make decisions quickly and without full information, with the next change requiring a decision before the first is fully implemented. They will need to take risks and not be afraid of occasional setbacks or failure. A manager recently described this as 'You cannot cross a swamp without falling in and getting mucky.' They will need to have a clear vision of the purpose of their organization, but demonstrate flexibility in how this is achieved. They will have to make decisions based on information received (feedback from the environment) and not be distracted by irritators (described as 'the flies and mosquitoes'). Above all they need to work in 'real time', not learning in theory or by case study but from doing, gaining feedback, testing assumptions and adapting their behaviour from that learning to meet new challenges.

If we accept that the features of managing in the future will include many of the above, then what are the implications for managerial skills?

ILLUSTRATION

A group of senior managers were asked 'What do you think will be the key features of effective management teams in the future?' Their response included the following features:

- Quick decision making.
- Innovative and forward looking.
- Risk taking.
- Creativity and resourcefulness.
- Responsive to change – flexible.
- Permission to make mistakes (once!).
- Outward looking.
- Effective at developing staff.
- Monitoring, reviewing and evaluating.
- Knowing when to stop.
- Committed.
- Effective use of modern technology.
- Client centred.
- High levels of negotiating and consultancy skills.
- High stress threshold.

The key managerial skills for the future

Managers of the future will need a wide range of skills. Obviously, we do not yet know all the answers, but using current management thinking and our work with a number of groups, we believe some of the more crucial skills will be the following:

1. Visioning and planning skills.
2. Information handling skills.
3. Influencing and negotiating skills.
4. Creativity and learning.
5. Team building and transformational leadership.

(See Figure 8.2 for an illustration of how these skills work together.)

1. Visioning and planning skills

In times of constant change, with changing roles and blurred organizational boundaries, it can be very difficult to have a clear view of

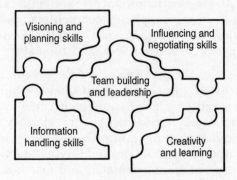

Figure 8.2 Five types of skill

the future of your organization or unit. However, without a sense of purpose and direction the energies of people at work can quickly become dissipated. So many people in organizations become demoralized and de-motivated if they feel that there is no one with a vision of, or commitment to, the future survival and growth of their business. Managers will need to generate a picture of the future, which includes a place for the organization and its staff. It may not be possible to support this vision, mission, or statement of purpose with detailed long-term plans in the same way as in the past, but providing a clear view of a future for the organization is crucial as a point of focus for staff. The skills to analyze the environment, the organization's strengths and weaknesses, options and consequences, together with skills in project and contingency planning, will enable you to translate the overall vision into operational reality. One of the barriers to doing this, however, may be the sheer volume of information available to you to choose from.

2. Information handling skills

One of the features of the IT revolution has been the massive increase in the amount of information which can now be generated at work. The problem is often not what to collect, but what to ignore. Clearly managers of the future will need to be comfortable using new technology to help them generate and manage the information they need. The following are three types of information which managers will need to be able to collect, interpret and use:

1. Information about and from the environment. At a broad level this means the political, economic, social and technological trends which might impact on the organization. More specifically it includes

information about the requirements and interests of customers, clients, fund holders, suppliers, competitors, politicians, and so forth; how these are changing; and the effect of those changes on demand for products and services, and the nature of relationships.

2. Information about the performance of the organization and her/his unit in particular. In order to respond rapidly to changing circumstances and customer requirements, the manager will need up-to-date information relating to the viability, capability and capacity of her/his team or teams. This would include data relating to income, outputs, costs and profitability; productivity; progress on current work; problems encountered and new initiatives planned.

3. Information about her/his teams and the individuals within them. This would include their hopes, aspirations, fears and limitations; their stages of development; need for support, and so forth.

In their missions and statements of values, many organizations espouse the view that 'people are our most valuable resource'. However, this is not always reflected in the way they treat their staff, who often feel that there is little apparent concern for the contribution that they (could) make. Having a primary focus outside the organization does not mean a manager can ignore the needs of individuals. On the contrary, in order to have an external focus, the manager needs to feel fully confident in the competence and commitment of every member of the team (see team building).

3. Influencing and negotiating skills

Managers have always needed influencing and negotiating skills, but when (i) the relationships with customers, suppliers, governments and other agencies are becoming more complex and (ii) the traditional hierarchical cultures are changing, managers will find themselves relying on these skills more and more as a central way of getting things done.

With increasingly complex networks of relationships between organizations, other agencies may have a greater say in the way you operate, the resources available to you or the deadlines you need to work to. In a climate of constant cutbacks you may need to negotiate with colleagues for your share of the available resources, and with changing expectations of working relationships you may need to rely on influencing and negotiating with colleagues and staff rather than relying on your expertise, position or other means, to make decisions and agree action. At the same time, both the external agencies and your staff may not share your objectives or perceptions of what is important, and consequently you may need to negotiate new ways of working together and to generate creative solutions in order to accommodate differing needs.

4. Creativity and learning

Creativity is another of the things that many organizations say they value, even require, from their managers, while at the same time they discourage or even ridicule new ideas. Nurturing creativity will mean that, in future, individuals at all levels of management will need to demonstrate that they are ready to accept challenges to the status quo and even to their own preferences. They may need to create a forum where experimentation, rather than risk aversion, is welcomed and where there is a more open attitude to making mistakes without losing respect. At a personal level, managers and staff may need help to develop or release ideas and to generate new options, or to produce creative solutions to problems which cannot be solved by traditional methods. This will have implications for the development of coaching and mentoring skills (see Chapter 7), so that individuals and teams can become more confident and competent and so become more self-managing.

5. Team building and transformational leadership

In the language of situational leadership a 'task mature' individual or team is one that is both highly competent and confident. This means that, in turn, a manager could confidently delegate to the team, leaving them to work on their own initiative, while s/he manages the boundary with the rest of the organization and the environment. In the past this might have seemed a goal to aim for, highly desirable but rather risky. We believe that in the future it will be essential. Managers will have no choice about taking an external focus, therefore they *must* be able to rely on their team(s) and trust them to function to quality assured standards with minimal support and supervision.

In the past, many companies have been more focused on tasks and results rather than team processes. Groups of people have been brought together and called teams but scant attention has been paid to actually developing teamwork to maximize both individual and collective potential. In contrast, self-managing teams will not only have to consistently perform to high standards but they will also have to be able to change and grow together as demands for their services change. This will require a special kind of leadership. There are many models of effective leadership. We believe that in the future the emphasis will need to be on a 'transformational' approach, where leaders not only mobilize commitment to enable performance today, they provide a vision for tomorrow and at the same time promote and facilitate change. As Hastings, Bixby and Chaudhry-Lawton (1986) identify, in future it is *Superteams* that may provide the blueprint for organizational success.

Thriving in a turbulent future

Although we believe that the development of the above skills will be crucial for managers in the future, doing so will not eliminate uncertainty and potential stress from the managerial role. On the contrary, sustaining a vision while not being certain how you will achieve it, processing vast quantities of varied data, working with different agencies to achieve negotiated solutions, fostering creativity and learning, and developing, then trusting, self-managing teams to deliver your product or service are all potentially threatening to your personal sense of security and well-being.

How do top managers maintain their health and well-being while at the same time remain successful at work? A recent study by Quick, Nelson and Quick (1990) of senior executives and professionals suggests there are the following five messages:

1. *Be intellectually curious.* Intellectual curiosity and education (formal or informal) expand a person's understanding of the world, providing perspective as well as knowledge for problem solving.

2. *Be physically active.* People who are physically active dissipate stress-induced energy while at the same time developing a stronger, more efficient cardiovascular system.

3. *Balance work with non-work.* People who balance work with non-work activities place their work in a larger, broader context of life which gives perspective and reduces psychological dependence.

4. *Seek social support.* Supportive relationships provide people with the means to meet a variety of their emotional, informational and evaluative needs, essential to healthy functioning.

5. *Create systematic change.* The people at the top need to be able to create an environment that is challenging, productive, creative and, at the same time, emotionally healthy.

Are there any alternatives?

How do you feel about this image of the future? Will you value the benefits of a managerial role? Will you thrive on the challenge of being a manager in the scenario we have painted? Or would you prefer an alternative? Our next and final chapter invites you to explore some of the alternatives.

Questionnaire: Preparing for managing in the future

1. Which of the following areas do you feel will have a significant impact on your organization in the future? And how?
    *   The environment.
    *   The shape of the organization.
    *   Your own role.
    *   The culture in the organization (the psychological contract).
    *   Individual and team development.
    *   Calculated risks and real-time learning.

What steps might you be able to take to influence your organization's preparations for working with these issues in the foreseeable future?

2. Which of the following skills do you feel (a) that you already have or (b) that you need to develop?
    *   Visioning and planning skills.
    *   Information handling skills.
    *   Influencing and negotiating skills.
    *   Creativity and learning.
    *   Team building and transformational leadership.

How might you plan to develop the ones that you need?

Chapter 9

Are there any other islands?

The future of work consists of learning *a living.*
(MARSHALL McLUHAN 1911–80)

Introduction

For some people the picture painted in the last chapter might be unappealing, unacceptable, frightening, or simply 'not for me'. If you are in this situation, you may feel that you do not want a future role in management for a number of reasons. For example, you may not have reached your full potential in your professional role or may not want to let go of things that this role offers you. You may consider that the potential benefits do not outweigh these losses. You may not be able to identify either sufficient stepping stones in your organization or the potential for lifelines. On the other hand, even if the kind of role that managers of the future are likely to have is unappealing, you may not have a choice. As the result of changes in your organization or industry, the expected career opportunities may not materialize because key roles will not be there in the future. This does not mean that there is no future but that you may need to develop a different approach to what that future might be.

To a great extent, perceptions about careers depend on the stage in the career that has been reached. At the end of a career you can look back and describe what has actually been achieved in concrete terms; it is very tangible. At the outset, however, a career is, to a large extent, in your head. It is the set of expectations you and others have of the future, for example, to have achieved X before you retire or to have made Y amount of money before you are forty.

In Chinese there is no single word which carries the same meaning as our word 'change'. Instead there are two words, one which would translate to 'threat', the other which means 'opportunity'. Maybe a change in your career plan is a real opportunity, it just needs to be seen as one.

In this chapter we would like to explore some of those opportunities. While it is not in any way intended to be an exhaustive list, it may give you some indications of a number of possible alternatives that would offer the kind of future you might be looking for.

What career paths are there?

Many people have told us that it is very difficult to return to a professional role, at least within the same organization. Equally, you may not have the choice of continuing along your current path. As Rosabeth Moss Kanter (1989) identified, with so many organizations going through major re-structuring, merging or changing direction, career patterns of people within them need to change too. She called it changing from 'climbing to hopping'. These organizational trends, together with economic recession, have also generated a fundamental shift to a more short-term perspective in employment practice, which is illustrated by the massive increase in the contracting out of work to self-employed individuals or small organizations. This means that there are no longer guarantees for individual roles. As Moss Kanter said, 'in the emerging workplace, opportunity goes to those who create the job, not those who inherit a predetermined set of tasks.'

How you feel about alternative careers will, to a large extent, depend on the stage you are at in your life and your career, when you are faced with making this change. Apart from the effect of such major events as marriage, parenthood and retirement, generally speaking, careers go through a number of stages.

In their research Arthur and Kram (1989) identified the following three stages:

1. *Exploring.* In this stage (which may last to the individual's mid-thirties), the person develops her/his competence at the job and forms an occupational identity. People in this stage learn a lot by doing, especially by performing technical or functional tasks, and often demonstrate a very high level of energy and exuberance.

2. *Directing.* Individuals at this stage have become clear about their career goals and preferences. For example, they may prefer managerial over technical roles and functions.

3. *Protecting.* By their mid- to late forties, most people try to secure and maintain their status, experience continued affirmation of their work, and pass on the benefits of their learning and experience to others.

In theory, each of these three stages builds on the other rather than replacing them. So individuals in the third stage expect their knowledge and experience to be put to good use; they want to maintain their role and status within society and their organization. This would make a major change in a career much more difficult for someone at this stage in the process than for someone in the first or second stages.

In a more specific study of scientists, engineers, accountants and academics, Dalton, Thompson and Price (1977) identified four career stages for these professionals:

1. *Apprenticeship* (age range from 21–60).
2. *Independence* (average age 41).
3. *Mentoring* (average age 41).
4. *Strategic responsibility* (average age 43).

In some organizations, only those designated 'manager' reached the third and fourth stages, while in others many non-managers did so. However, of those designated 'professionals' at the fourth stage, 75 per cent were, strictly speaking, ex-professionals since they had become general managers, or had directed key organizational programmes, sponsored or invented a new product, or provided a new set of ideas which affected the company as a whole.

So while on the one hand professionals in their late forties may feel very protective of their profession, those who had attained the higher levels of career development, had also moved away from the profession into management.

Clark (1992) used pictures to identify a number of different career models including the following:

- Triangle and ladder models, where every employee or manager enters the organization at the same hierarchical level and gradually works her/his way up in a direct line along the pyramid.
- The spiral model, where employees are required to move laterally into different functional roles before being promoted to the next level in the organization.
- The pyramid model, which assumes that there is always some advancement through climbing up a recognized organizational hierarchy (although this has been undermined because of the sort of organizational changes already mentioned).
- The roller coaster model, which is a more recent model, reflects the greater uncertainties generated by rapid organizational change. Here, careers move both vertically and horizontally at varying speed and levels, and since the roller coaster is changing direction and speed so often, the route and destination are not always clear to the passengers.

Which of these have you followed (or perceived for yourself) to date? If your perspective has now changed, what might be possible in the future?

What are the alternatives?

1. Specialist niche: Internal consultant

If in the future 'opportunity goes to those who create the job' is there a new professional role which you can develop, and which offers you a viable alternative to continue to use and develop your professional skills? Using Arthur and Kram's model, if you are in the 'protecting' stage of your career, it may be that you have to change organizations, but could continue to practise your profession in the way that you wish. Dalton, Thompson and Price suggest that you may be able to work in a mentoring or strategic role by taking responsibility for a special project or becoming an internal consultant. If this is unlikely within your own organization, it may be possible in another one or as part of a professional association or academic institution. Alternatively, independence may be possible by establishing your own organization, networking with other professionals or joining a small 'professional practice' providing specialist advise and help.

2. Retirement/early retirement/voluntary redundancy

If you have reached the later stages in you career, you may have developed a sense that you have 'had enough'. As a result you may be considering retirement. For example, if you have worked for many years and seen many changes, you may not want to go through any more and decide to retire. Furthermore, if you are in an acceptable position financially, you may decide to hasten the process and retire before it is necessary. Early retirement may provide an attractive alternative, especially if the organization you work for offers enhanced terms for your pension which would give you the opportunity to do a number of things you currently do not have time for. However, you may wish to take time to reflect on what work has really meant to you. As we explored in Chapter 3 a professional role provides much more than a job of work; work itself also provides structure and purpose to our lives.

What does a job give you?
As Bridges (1994) points out, a job has several meanings:

1. It helps people to *tell themselves and others who they are*. In past village and tribal societies, identity was established by birth. Who you are was one of life's givens. In a modern society that is not the case; no one can say at birth who individuals will turn out to be. People build their own identities from their friends, their family life, the activities they pursue, the schools and churches they attend – and the jobs they have. Especially the jobs. As we have already mentioned, when people meet for the first time, they define who they are by what they do and frequently talk to each other about work.

2. It also provides most people with their *core network of relationships*. Whether or not their co-workers are good friends (and that is not uncommon), for most people the job is the main social context of their lives. It is where they belong. Even if they don't like everyone there, the other people become part of their lives. If any individual loses her/his job, these people all disappear. Without a job, life can feel both flat and lonely.

3. A job has a *time structure* to it, without which life can feel as 'vast and empty as outer space'. The working day provides a structure, such as starting at 9 a.m. and finishing at 5 p.m., with a set period of time for lunch. The phone rings and you have to pick it up by the fourth ring or it transfers to someone else. The mail comes and goes at given times. There are eight statutory holidays a year and a set amount of annual holiday. Their job gives a pattern to the days, weeks and years of people's lives. 'It makes living – a confusing business at best – more predictable.' Without a job, time can stretch endlessly.

4. A job gives people *parts to play* and tells them what they need to do to feel good about their contribution. It gives them a way of knowing when they have done enough, and it tells them when their results are satisfactory. Jobs provide people with a place where they need to show up regularly; a list of things they have got to do; a role to play in some larger undertaking; and a set of expectations to be measured against. It gives them an everyday sense of purpose. And fulfilling such purpose is a source of self-esteem. For people whose personal lives are not going very well, the job may be the only source of self-esteem.

In short, for most people, a job is a primary source of meaning and order in their lives. If this is true for you, how would you feel without it? Many people reach retirement and feel lost. How would you fill your days? What else would provide you with a sense of purpose and identity?

Voluntary redundancy may be another alternative. In considering this option it would be important to weigh up the costs and benefits of volunteering, and whether your employer would allow you to go. This may seem to be a very attractive option, especially if the terms are favourable or the pressures (such as poor health or difficult family circumstances) are high. The freedom of not having to go to work can seem very attractive, but if your main motivation is 'to get out' rather than 'to move on' it may be useful to consider what you will do instead. The options include the alternatives which follow in this chapter.

3. Transfer to another employer

If it is difficult to stay in, or return to, a professional role in the same organization without feeling a loss of status, then it may be possible to transfer to another employer, possibly in another location or even another country. It is very common for individuals to find that they need to leave their employer and 'hop' in order to develop their career. However, while this may be a major option, the range of opportunities will depend on the buoyancy of the economy. In times of economic recession changing job and moving house might be very difficult or unattractive. On the other hand, there may be tremendous opportunities if you are prepared to move to another country, where your professional skills are needed and will be valued. Given your personal circumstances, is this a viable option for you?

4. Contracting your services: Becoming self-employed

As we have identified, this appears to be a major trend. You may not feel able to return to, or develop in, your professional base within the same organization, but you may be able to 'freelance' or work on a contracted basis for one or more organizations. In effect, this means becoming self-employed. Many people have taken this route already and there are clearly real advantages in working for yourself. These include the following:

- A much greater control over your own working arrangements. What to do, when to do it, where to be based and how much work to seek and do.
- The opportunity to work with a variety of people and organizations.
- The ability to focus on your own work and interests without being drawn into office 'politics'.
- The chance for continuous development – to build the areas of work and skills that you are most interested in and not to get distracted by other (organizational) activities.

However, there are also a number of disadvantages such as the following:

- Starting up a new business is time consuming and can be both costly and risky, depending on the status you choose. You may decide to work independently, in a network of colleagues or in a more formal business arrangement with other people, such as a partnership or by establishing a limited company.
- As well as taking responsibility for the marketing and delivery of all aspects of your services, this will also mean setting up accounting systems and being responsible for your own taxation, pension, health care, transport, and so forth.
- You may not be able to choose your work. There may not be a regular or sufficient flow of work. Many self-employed people use the expression that 'it is always feast or famine'.
- Working alone can also be very lonely. If, as Bridges identified, one of the things that work provides is a 'core network of relationships', then, conversely, being self-employed can mean that you do not have any colleagues, only customers.
- You may be able to secure one major, long-term contract or have several smaller ones, but there will always be a degree of uncertainty about the longer term future. So, if uncertainty and the lack of security are two of the features of being a manager in the future which you find unappealing, then this option may be no more attractive.

5. Training or consultancy

It may be that you are able to share your knowledge and experience by taking on a training or consultancy role within your professional field. This could be within your current organization, with a new employer, with a professional association or academic institution, or on a self-employed basis.

The features of transferring to another employer, or becoming self-employed would still apply, but there is another key dimension to this alternative. Not everyone who is good at what they do is interested in, or good at, helping others to develop the same expertise. A number of people see training as an easy option, but to be really effective in this role takes as much personal development as any other profession. Skilled trainers need the following:

- Highly developed planning, organizing and communication skills.
- Patience, creativity and resilience.

- A very strong commitment to coaching and enabling others to develop their potential.

Unless you share these drives, training can be a very frustrating experience.

Similarly, it has been said that consultants are 'people that charge you a great deal of money to tell you what you already know'. This particularly negative view of what is a very diverse profession seems to have developed at the same time as a dramatic increase in consultancy activity and establishment of firms offering consultancy services. How a consultant operates will depend on the nature of the services s/he provides. A technically-based problem or change will often require the consultant to use their knowledge and expertise directly, in order to explore the issues and suggest solutions. However, if the nature of the work is concerned with interpersonal and organizational processes, success will depend much more on the consultant's ability to work with the interests and motivations of the client. In either case it will be the client's role to implement any recommendations that are made, and the consultant must learn to 'let go' of a project when it has reached a logical conclusion. Skilled consultants need the following:

- Highly developed planning, organizing and communication skills.
- Patience, creativity and resilience.
- Political sensitivity and experience of how organizations work.
- An understanding of the consulting cycle.
- Project management skills.
- The ability to work closely with people and yet remain objective.
- The ability to finish an assignment and leave on a positive note.

6. A new career

This may seem like the most exciting (or dangerous) alternative; it is certainly the most radical. (As the Monty Python comedy team would say, 'Now for something completely different.') We recognize that although in the past many people at the outset of their working lives have expected to build their career in that one field of work, it is becoming increasingly necessary for them to consider changing careers once or more than once during their working lives. One of the features of rapid economic change is the changing demand for skills as well as more flexible working patterns.

What else might you do? Have you interests, hobbies or talents which are not currently utilized in your working life? Is there something you have always wanted to do but never had the chance to? Have you developed new skills in the past few years or an interest in a completely new occupation? Maybe this is your opportunity for a whole new beginning.

In this book we are not able to explore these alternatives in great detail. Your specific options will depend on your own personal situation. However, we would like to suggest a way of exploring the issues before you decide.

How to decide?

We believe that there are three key elements to exploring the options in order to set the direction for your future. They are as follows:

1. *Values*. What are your personal values, and how would these affect the significant features of an ideal future?
2. *Needs*. What are your fundamental needs? The things that are essential for your personal well-being, lifestyle and work satisfaction?
3. *Opportunities*. What opportunities can you create to open doors for the future?

What are values?

Values are the bedrock of how we live our lives. They underpin how we think, what we do, and how we make decisions. They are the source of our motivation and failure to satisfy them can generate frustration and stress.

There is some disagreement about the source of personal values. Some researchers argue that they are inherited and others that they develop during our formative years, while another group would suggest that they develop in response to the demands of the various stages in our lives. We believe that there is probably a mixture. Some values are a fundamental part of our personality and others develop as the result of significant influences and life experiences. For example, most people would argue that they value good health, but many do not show much concern for their diet, exercise and lifestyle until a major illness makes them focus on their health.

The fundamental values would include things such as freedom, integrity and loyalty to other people. Other values are instrumental: they are the means to an end. For example, a promotion may be valued not for itself but because it represents greater freedom or recognition. It is crucial that your personal values have some measure of congruence with those of your organization or work style, as a serious mismatch can lead to unhappiness, frustration and stress. For example, if you value loyalty and recognition of people but work for an organization that seems to value profit to the exclusion of caring for its employees, it would probably lead to personal unhappiness or frustration.

What are your values?

In exploring your own values it may be helpful to distinguish fundamental and instrumental values, and then relate these to the possible alternative futures. If you value freedom, a measure of control over your own work would be important and becoming a contractor or self-employed would match that need. If you value security, however, it would probably be better to seek an alternative source of permanent employment. If you value solitude and self-reliance, again, working alone would generate enjoyment, but if you value being part of a team (a sense of community), then working with others would be important to your well-being.

What are your needs?

There are also two types of need – the essential and the tradeable. The essentials are things that you consider to be essential to work and life. The health and well-being of yourself and your family, a level of economic security, a particular type of home, a job that you enjoy doing, and so forth. The tradeables are those things that you would be willing to exchange or forego for something you value more. For example, would you trade economic security for an adventure? A promotion for a job that you enjoy doing? Or a job that you enjoy for greater recognition?

Many employers whose organizations are located in beautiful areas find that staff will stay in a role longer than they had anticipated, not because they do not want promotion, but because they value more highly the opportunities to explore the countryside in their non-working hours.

What are your opportunities?

Opportunities are the things that you would really like to aim for. What would you like to do given the opportunity? Can you create your own opportunities? Do you set limits on yourself? Have challenges from other people meant that you set limits on what you believe you are capable of?

While you may have something in mind, you may also tell yourself that it is an ideal and not at all realistic. We believe it is important not to set unnecessary limitations on yourself. We have only to look at the achievements of our heroes, those courageous individuals who achieve their goals in the face of immense difficulties, to realize there is truth in the saying 'there is nothing you cannot achieve if you want it hard enough.'

We would also ask you to question what really are *your* values rather than the things you feel you should value because other people have in the past, or still do, put pressure on you.

If you are in any doubt about this, think about your actions not words. For example, do you say you value family bonds but know that you regularly forget birthdays? Do you say that you value security but really yearn for an adventure? Ask yourself the question: *What do I really want?*

Activity: Seven steps to the future

---

1. Make a list of your values.
   The following examples may help:

Integrity	Spirituality	Freedom
Loyalty	Achievement	Personal growth
Self-respect	Recognition	Creativity
Power	Happiness	Good health
Physical safety	Affection/friendship/love	

   ...
   ...
   ...
   ...
   ...

2. Identify your needs. It may help to think of them not in absolute terms but as a hierarchy. (For example, if you have prime responsibility for the care of other relatives, a level of economic security may be a must and job enjoyment a want; but if you are responsible only for yourself, the needs may be ranked the other way around.)
   The following list may help you:

Economic security	Achievement	Advancement
Status	Recognition	Responsibility

   ...
   ...
   ...

   MUSTS – to maintain or protect

WANTS – to increase

LIKES – ideals or tradables

3. Identify the features of life and work that are more or less important to you. Using the following factors, locate yourself along each of these scales.

Certainty	Challenge
Consistency	Variety
Solitude	Involvement
Responsibility	Freedom
Strategic planning	Trouble shooting
Long time scales	Short time scales
Deadlines	Open ended
Order	Adventure
Staying put	Travel
Relaxation	Physical activity
Steady work	Bursts of activity
Planned activity	Spontaneity
Interdependence	Independence
Being led	Leading others
Co-operation	Competition
Routine	Change
Predictability	Uncertainty
Unobtrusiveness	Fame/status
Intellectual challenge	Intellectual comfort
....	....
....	....

4. Think of your life as a continuous journey and make a map of your journey to date, identifying the events that have had a positive effect on you and those which have had a negative effect (the highs and lows). Figure 9.1 maps out the possible futures on a sample journey. Note that some things may have aspects of both and so would appear both above and below the line on your map.

5. Using the information generated so far, can you identify any pattern to the events? Can you do anything to enhance the positive and minimize the negative aspects?

6. Can you also identify the key features of your possible futures? What directions could you take?

7. What might your alternative island look like? Does it provide for your long-term needs or the basis for further travel? Can you draw it?

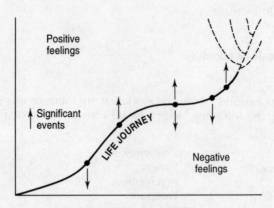

Figure 9.1   Possible futures

We invite you to make your own opportunities, take the challenge and build what you want from life. Whatever your future looks like, we wish you an exciting and enjoyable journey. In the words of Robert Browning, 'Ah but man's reach should exceed his grasp, else what's a heaven for?'

References

Arthur, M. and Kram, K. (1989) 'Reciprocity at work: the separate, yet inseparable possibilities for individual and organisational development', in Arthur, M., Hall, D. and Lawrence, B. (eds) *Handbook of Career Theory*, Cambridge: Cambridge University Press.

Bridges, W. (1994) *Job Shift: How to Prosper in a Workplace Without Jobs*, Reading: Addison-Wesley.

Casey, D. and Pearce, D.W. (1977) *More than Management Development*, Farnborough: Gower Press.

Clark, F. (1992) *Total Career Management*, London: McGraw-Hill.

Clifton, D.O. and Nelson, P. (1992) *Play to Your Strengths*, London: BCA by arrangement with Judy Piatkus (Publishers) Ltd.

Cox, C. and Cooper, C. (1988) *High Flyers*, Oxford: Basil Blackwell.

Dalton, P., Thompson P. and Price, R. (1977) 'The four stages of professional careers', *Organisational Dynamics*, Summer: 19–42.

Evans, P. (1991) *Motivation revisited: striking a dynamic balance in the dualist organisation*, Barcelona: Management Centre Europe.

Handy, C. (1994) *The Empty Raincoat*, London: Hutchinson.

Hastings, C., Bixby, P. and Chaudhry-Lawton, R. (1986) *Superteams*. Farnborough: Gower Press.

Hersey, P. and Blanchard, K. (1988) *Management of Organisational Behaviour: Utilising Human Resources*. Englewood Cliffs, NJ: Prentice Hall.

Herzberg, F., Mousiner, B. and Snyderman, B.B. (1959) *The Motivation to Work*, New York: J. Wiley and Sons.

Hiltrop, J. (1995) 'The changing psychological contract: the human resource issues of the 1990s?', *European Management Journal*, Vol 13, No. 3, pp 286–94.

Kolb, D. A. (1984) *Experiential Learning, Experience as a Source of Learning and Development*, Englewood Cliffs, NJ: Prentice Hall.

Mintzberg, H. (1973) *The Nature of Managerial Work*, New York: Harper and Row.

Morgan, G. (1988) *Riding the Waves of Change*, San Francisco, CA: Jossey-Bass.

Moss Kanter, R. (1989) *When Giants Learn to Dance*, London: Simon & Schuster.

Nicholson, N. and West, A. (1988) *Managerial Job Change: Men and Women in Transition*, Cambridge: Cambridge University Press.

123

Peters, T. and Quinn, R. (1988) *Beyond Rational Management*, New York: Jossey-Bass.

Quick, J., Nelson, D. and Quick, J. (1990) *Stress and Challenge at the Top: The Paradox of the Successful Executive*, New York: John Wiley & Sons.

Rousseau, D. and Greller, M. (1994) 'Human resource practices: administrative contract makers', *Human Resource Management*, Fall 1994, Vol 33, No. 3, pp 385–402.

Scase, R. and Goffee, R. (1989) *Reluctant Managers*, London: Unwin Hyman.

Sparrow, P. and Boam, R. (1992) *Focusing on Human Resources: a competency-based approach*, London: McGraw-Hill.

White, B., Cox, C. and Cooper, C. (1992) *Women's Career Development*, Cambridge: Blackwell Publishers.

Index